Volume I

FORTITUDE
True Stories of True Grit

edited by Malinda Teel

Red Rock Press   New York

ISBN: 0-9669573-7-7
Library of Congress: 00-190830

Published by Red Rock Press
459 Columbus Avenue, Suite 114
New York, New York 10024
U.S.A.
www.redrockpress.com

"Lost in the Wilderness" by Garry Cooper is adapted, by permission, from an article published in the July/August 1996 issue of *The Family Therapy Networker*, 8528 Bradford Road, Silver Spring, MD 20901.

"Sailor Alone in a Wild Sea" by Derek Lundy first appeared in the January 1999 issue of *The Algonkian*, ©1998 by Algonquin Books of Chapel Hill.

"Eyes Wide Open or Else!" is reprinted with the permission of Scribner, a Division of Simon & Schuster, from *The Spirit of St. Louis* by Charles Lindbergh. Copyright ©1953 by Charles Scribner's Sons; copyright renewed ©1981 by Anne Morrow Lindbergh.

"Death Was Our Escort" is reprinted with the permission of Simon & Schuster from *Death Was Our Escort* by Ernest Vetter, Copyright ©1944 by Prentice-Hall, Inc., renewed 1972.

"The Receiver Who Refused to Quit" is excerpted from *The Greatest Sports Stories Never Told*, by Bruce Nash and Allan Zullo. Published by Simon & Schuster, ©1993. Reprinted by permission of Nash & Zullo Productions, Inc.

"The Prayer" is reprinted from *The Faithful Gardener: A Wise Tale About That Which Can Never Die*, by Clarissa Pinkola Estés, Ph.D., Copyright ©1995. All rights reserved. Reprinted by kind permission of Dr. Estés and HarperCollins Publishers, Inc.

"This Was My Best,That Day" is published here with permission of Louis Parrillo, Jr. © Louis Parrillo, Jr.

Virtue Victorious angel by Barbara Swanson

Back cover art: *The Rocky Mountains*, Currier & Ives

Cover design by Kathleen Herlihy-Paoli

Book design by Paul Perlow

Printed in the United States

TO TOM AND SAM

Thank you, Sam, for putting up with a distracted Mom.
Tom, my love, you have supported me in a thousand
different ways. I will always be grateful.

THANK YOU

I'm grateful to the following people: Julie Ziercher and George Mitchell, who helped me decide to do this book; Bill Pfeiffer and Lana Hardy, who taught me to navigate the Internet; John Liles and Fred Wolters, who rescued me from my computer's attempts at sabotage; Susan Formby, who let me cry on her shoulder and offered last-minute copyediting help; Ernestine Selby, who shared her Internet research; and Nancy Haber and Stephanie Ezust, who gave me input on stories.

Thanks to the following folks who suggested people for me to talk to, sent authors my way or shared material with me: Dina Zeckhausen, Jim Winship, Bob Lupton, Wendy Patterson, Connie Curry, Karen Fisher, Stephen Wing, Renelle Massey, Mary Logan, Kathy Bruss, Rosemerry Trommer, Mary Ann Navarre, Sally Lehr, Debra Greenwood, Josh Frank, Roland Caissie, Iris Bolton, Jeffry Gallet, Chris Martin, Jane Roughton, Richard Bondi, Sandra West, Alexa Selph, Sarah Rick, Betsy Johnson, Mary Mannhardt, Holly Morris, Janet LaBrie, Ann Perrelli of the Atlanta Peace Corps Office, Leslie Credit of the American Red Cross, Leslie Levy at Atlanta's Jewish Family and

Career Services, and the Georgia Advocacy Office. Even if your suggestions or material didn't make their way into the book, your support meant a lot to me.

In addition, I am appreciative of Eleanor Brownfield, whose popcorn-popper mind came through; the librarians at the Georgia-Hill branch of the Atlantic Public Library, who were unfailingly courteous and helpful; Lock McLendon, my Scottish connection; Paul Fair, who reminded me to breathe; Ron Hussey, at Simon & Schuster, who let me "butt in line" to get last-minute permission to reprint a piece; Alex Toth, archivist at Pacific University; Jim Hasse (www.tell-us-your-story.com/top.html); and Larry Stevens, whose transcription of a Civil War veteran's memory I found on his web site (my.ohio.voyager.net/~lstevens/a/civil.html).

Special thanks to my authors and interviewees, delightful collaborators all; and to Ilene Barth, who gave me the chance to do this book, shared her knowledge, encouragement, and resources generously, and had faith in me when I wavered.—M.T.

TO BE HUMAN IS TO BE BRAVE

Fortitude is a funny thing. It's easy to talk oneself out of its existence, attributing courageous endurance instead to adrenaline or a person's cockeyed denial of the enormity of the difficulties facing him or her. In talking about their own fortitude, people sometimes shrug it off with a phrase I heard often while doing this book: "I had no choice but to act as I did." But the fact remains that some people meet challenges and danger in heroic ways, and their stories inspire us to do better. I know this from recent experience. Even though creating a book ranks low on the fortitude scale, I had dark moments when I questioned whether I would ever accomplish what I'd set out to do. At those times, calling to mind the subjects of the stories I was collecting helped pull me through.

Greek philosophers viewed fortitude as a manly virtue, military in nature. Plato, for instance, saw fortitude as a toughness to be acquired so that suffering and death in battle might be bravely faced. Aristotle, thinking also of warfare, emphasized that some active display of valor—as on the battlefield—was intrinsic to fortitude.

Centuries later, St. Ambrose moved the concept of fortitude into the moral arena, describing it as bravery in facing dangers and temptations while waging war on vice. His student, St. Augustine, enlarged the scope of fortitude to mean enduring any misfortune or grief. In the 13th century, St. Thomas Aquinas devoted several pages in his *Summa Theologica* to a discussion of fortitude, ranking it third in importance among the virtues, behind prudence and justice, reasoning that "the greatness of a virtue is measured according to its goodness rather than its difficulty." St. Thomas wrestled with such questions as whether fortitude occurs only in battle and only when one faces the danger of death, as well as whether the passive endurance of the martyrs was a match for the active fortitude of the warrior.

In creating this collection, I have not been concerned with such philosophical hair-splitting, and have opted for the broadest possible definition of fortitude. Fortitude, in my book, is courage, strength, perseverance, and/or patience in the face of difficulty, with a connotation of persistence over time. It may involve inner struggles as well as external adversity. Its other names include "true grit," "fighting the good fight," "staying the course," "valor," and "stout-heartedness."

It is my belief that almost everyone has some measure of fortitude. Life has a habit of requiring it. This book is a celebration of the fortitude in us all.

—Malinda Teel
Atlanta, Georgia

TABLE OF CONTENTS

SECTION I

◆ BRAVING THE ELEMENTS ◆

*"We are made to persist.
That's how we find out who we are."*
—TOBIAS WOLFF

LOST IN THE WILDERNESS
Garry Cooper

One summer night a few years back, I had to decide whether to live through the night or let myself die. I had been lost in New Mexico's Pecos Wilderness for several days. I had dropped about 10 pounds, the night was cold, my shoes and socks were soaked and my toes had blistered so deeply they were numb. I started shivering, the first symptom of life-threatening hypothermia. Dying began to seem as appealing as going to sleep under a goose-down comforter. The only troubling question was whether the shivering would be terrible for a long time or whether I would pass through it quickly.

Every year I go on a solitary backpacking trip. That year I had hired a wrangler for the uphill climb into the mountains. He took both horses back, leaving me to hike alone and eventually make my own way out. Unused to horseback riding, I'd strained a groin muscle and instead of healing, over the next few days it got worse, making walking more and more painful. When I realized I was lost, I knew that staying put was the best strategy. But I felt time pressure—I was overdue for a conference in Santa Fe. More important, I'd promised my four-year-old daughter that I'd call Saturday night, two nights past. After some desperate wandering I found a trail that I thought would lead within a few hours to a populated campground. My injury felt so close to herniating that I decided to travel light. In the interest of speed, I shucked my tent and sleeping bag.

Three hours later I came to a shallow river, which I believed stood between me and the campground. However, cliffs and rock formations forced me to keep crisscrossing the river that started running deeper and faster. In the middle of a crossing I stepped into a sinkhole, sank to my waist and fell. The fast waters started to sweep me downstream. Frantic, I managed to right myself and struggle to the shore. The contents of my backpack were soaked and useless, so I threw it away. By now I realized I had badly miscalculated—safety was miles away. It was evident that a thunderstorm was imminent. Pressing myself against a cliff with an overhang, I wrote a good-bye letter to my wife on the back of a wallet-size photo. When the storm broke it was fierce.

That night I covered myself with piles of pine branches. I spent the next two days alternately climbing to the top of a mountain so a search plane could see me and climbing down to the river for water. But pain, lack of food and exhaustion took their toll. The climbs took longer and longer, and my mind started drifting. I heard automobile horns, as cruel a hallucination as seeing a mirage oasis in a desert. Stumbling toward a cactus I hoped to eat, I got distracted watching an eagle soar across the sky and passed the cactus. Later that afternoon I got caught in a hailstorm. Suddenly, it was night and the temperature had plummeted. Disoriented and unable to find my cache of branches, I was without cover of any sort.

I found myself wringing my hands and preparing to die.

Then I thought of my four-year-old daughter, or rather, I felt her, inside my chest. I imagined her experiencing my disappearance forever, without a good-bye. I would have given my soul to appear before her for one minute just to tell her that although I was going to die, sometimes she would still be able to close her eyes and see me. I wanted to reassure her, for I understood she'd never feel safe again. I thought of her flinching every time she began to feel hope or love. Her face floated in the thin mountain air like a hologram, and I watched her expression melt from innocence into fear. I squeezed my eyes shut. Suddenly I realized my hands were no longer wringing; they were rubbing. Then I began to rub them briskly. "I can't die," I said aloud. "I'm not going to die."

I took my small hunting knife and began digging a trench, muttering over and over, "I'm not going to die." I worked steadily, completely focused. I placed every good-sized stone that I dug out just beyond the growing pile of dirt, so that once I had packed myself in the trench, I could reach them and build a windbreak. Finally, I climbed in, bending my legs to fit and—yes—it occurred to me that the trench might end up a grave. I piled the dirt on top of myself, leaving one arm free to build the stone windbreak.

When I had finished, the shivering began again, consuming precious energy. I knew I had to keep it under control or die. Then I remembered my yoga from over 20 years ago, and I began deep breathing and chanting, "Ommmm." Soon the shivering slowed, then stopped. After a while the deep breathing and chanting acquired their own rhythm; it took less exertion to continue than to stop.

I have always had this problem when backpacking: By the time the stars come out, it is too cold to lean back and leisurely contemplate them. I have berated myself for not going outside and doing what I did 40 years ago as a child: Lie on my back and stare up into the vast night sky until a pleasant dizziness takes hold. But when I decided to live, on that midsummer night in the Pecos Wilderness, lying packed in dirt, breathing in the night air and chanting out toward the stars, I came as close to paradise as I will ever come. Up in the night sky, a search plane buzzed and blinked, like a blind angel. The plane, like my chanting, was just another part of the great panorama.

They found me the next afternoon through an extraordinary piece of luck. I had staggered down toward the river at the precise moment a search team was walking along the opposite

> *"Courage is resistance to fear, mastery of fear—not absence of fear." Consider the flea!—incomparably the bravest of all the creatures of God, if ignorance of fear were courage. Whether you are asleep or awake he will attack you, caring nothing for the fact that in bulk and strength you are to him as are the massed armies of the earth to a sucking child."*
>
> —Mark Twain

bank. We could not see each other, but they were calling my name loudly enough for me to hear it over the river's roar. I had time and energy for only one good shout. I took a deep breath and shouted, "Here!"

In a moment, four people were thrashing through the water, setting off a smoke flare and shouting into radios. It was like an ambush of mercy.

Looking back on that experience, I believe that love, a thing greater than myself, saved me. And now that I've felt this kind of love, I think about my life differently. I expect that I will spend the rest of my life remembering that moment in the wilderness, honoring it and searching for it again.

Garry Cooper is a therapist in Oak Park, Illinois.

TRAPPED IN THE ARCTIC

L incoln Ellsworth had dreamed all his life of going to the North Pole and, at age 45, he got his chance. Even better, he was teamed up with his hero, Norwegian explorer Roald Amundsen, the first person to have set foot on the South Pole. Ellsworth had earned a place on Amundsen's team by lining up funding. The Amundsen group hoped to be the first to fly over the North Pole; they also wanted to reach it on foot.

On May 21, 1925, Ellsworth, Amundsen and four others set off from Spitzbergen, an island in the Greenland Sea, in two small seaplanes with open cockpits. After flying 600 miles and using half their fuel, the pilots began their descent, believing they were close to the North Pole—although they had actually drifted 156 miles off course. The terrain below was a patchwork of small ice floes, strewn with an obstacle course of ice forms— blocks of ice, hills of ice, and wall-like ice ridges as tall as houses.

Both planes miraculously escaped damage as they landed but were trapped in different icy channels. The explorers were cut off from the rest of the world, with only a month's supply of food. Ellsworth and his pilot, Dietrichson, were able to spot Amundson's plane from the top of an ice hill; getting to it was another matter. Ellsworth's threesome, which included the mechanic, Omdal, wore or carried wooden cross-country skis (depending on the terrain) as they fought their way over crevasses and up and down icebergs only to find their progress checked by a wide, impassable channel. Over the next three days, Ellsworth and his companions toiled to haul their plane onto solid ice. Then they again resolved to reach Amundsen. This time they elected a winding route around ridges and hummocks. Seven hours later, they returned to their camp, thwarted again by a wide lead, covered by a dangerously thin crust of ice.

A frigid wind had begun blasting across the Arctic wasteland, and on the morning of May 26, Ellsworth and his companions found their ice floe blown within a half-mile of Amundsen. Furthermore, the channels had frozen more solidly. Would the new ice now be thick enough to support them? They decided to chance it, and started across the lead—first Omdal, then Ellsworth, then Dietrichson.

Suddenly the ice gave way beneath Omdal and Dietrichson, and they disappeared from view. Ellsworth, feeling the ice sag, jumped quickly sideways onto a ledge of old ice. Dietrichson's head bobbed up above the water. Ellsworth quickly shook off his skis. Lying on his stomach, he held them out to Dietrichson, and as the pilot clung to the skis, Ellsworth managed to drag him onto solid ice.

Omdal had also surfaced. "I'm gone! I'm gone!" he cried desperately, digging his fingers into the ice as he felt the current pulling him down again. Ellsworth grabbed Omdal's pack and held up the nearly unconscious man until Dietrichson joined them. With their last remaining strength, the two dragged Omdal to safety. Then all three struggled on to Amundsen's camp.

Reunited, the six men faced the task of chopping Amundsen's plane out of the ice that had frozen around it. They would also have to haul it onto the floe and position it for takeoff, as well as hack through icebergs to make a runway. In the course of their efforts, Amundsen estimated, they moved 500 tons of ice. Finally, on the 25th day after landing, the seaplane, with all six men aboard, took flight and headed back to civilization.

"One would naturally think after such an experience that we had had enough," Ellsworth later wrote. "But no, our work was not yet finished. Beyond—to the northward—still stretched the unknown." The following year, Ellsworth and Amundsen were back at it, this time in a dirigible airship. And this time, they successfully crossed over the North Pole.

RETURNING TO THE RIVER OF NO RETURN
Rosemerry Wahtola Trommer

I nearly drowned when I was 12. It happened on the Salmon River, in Idaho, where I was rafting with my friend Lara and her family. Lara and I were paddling a small kayak when we flipped. We'd flipped plenty of times before, but this time the river sucked me down toward the bottom and held me there, static. I remember looking toward the surface, watching the sunlight filter through murky swirls, and thinking, *So this is what it's like to die.* Then suddenly the river released me to the roiling surface, and I struggled toward shore through crashing waves. When I climbed out, I was bruised, scarred, and scared—but alive.

The next day Lara and I were back in our boat, laughing amidst the Salmon waves. But ever since that incident, I have dreamt of drowning several times a year. And in my dreams, the river doesn't spit me out.

Now, it is 1996, 14 years after my near-drowning, and I'm preparing for the Salmon again, this time with my husband, Eric, and a group of 16 friends. Despite my terror-filled dreams, running rivers remains one of my favorite things to do. Every summer, Eric and I take a couple of trips in our cataraft. After a day or two, we forget our workaday lives and remember all the reasons we're in love. We connect to the water, landscape and sky.

This trip we had planned to put in near Stanley, Idaho, running the Middle Fork of the Salmon before joining the Main Salmon. Even at its best, the Middle Fork is challenging: That's how it earned its moniker, "The River of No Return." Unfortunately, this second day of June, conditions are very bad. We arrive in Stanley to find that the river is running at flood levels, due to big snows and a late thaw. And the boat launch is buried under several feet of snow. Most private trips like ours have cancelled.

Local guides tell us that the swollen Middle Fork is dangerous and unpredictable—but do-able for seasoned boaters; and we can charter a plane to get to a snow-free launch 25 miles south. All of us are strong on experience, but none of us has ever been on a river in flood stage. We gather in a circle at base camp, and comments fly as members of the group discuss whether to proceed.

"Man, it was a 24-hour drive to get here. I say we go for it."

"I dunno, I kinda like living. Is it really worth it?"

"This will be epic. Did we bring enough beer?"

As the others banter, I remain subdued and silent, images from my watery nightmares floating through my mind. Fortitude be damned; I'm scared. Part of me just wants to drive back to Colorado. But everyone else seems gung-ho about continuing the trip. I allow myself to be influenced by their enthusiasm and say nothing about my fear. The die is cast: In two days, we'll run the river.

The following day, planes deposit us at Indian Creek, where we will put in the next morning. After unloading our supplies and six boats, ranging in size from a kayak to a four-person raft, we get our first look at the river. Trees stand in the water several feet out from shoreline. The campsite is under water. A small, furry carcass floats by. We watch in silence, then the chatter begins.

"I've never seen a river movin' so fast."

"Did you see the size of that log that went by?"

"I thought this river ran clear. It looks like chocolate milk."

"Does anyone know where the grub is?"

I feel a potato-sized lump rise in my throat. It keeps me from eating much dinner. Not even a Budweiser washes it down. Nor does a second one. When I wake up the next morning, it's still there.

LIFE AFTER THE WAGON TRAIN

Tabitha Brown was 66 when she set out on the Oregon Trail. In the spring of 1846, when she pulled up roots in Missouri to join a wagon train bound west, she was sure she was equal to the hardships of the journey. Little did she dream what trials lay in wait. Her real troubles in reaching Oregon began when she and a number of her fellow travelers were persuaded by a stranger to take a shortcut. This so-called shortcut led them far off course, through desolate, nearly impassable areas of present-day Nevada and California. Many emigrants died of hunger or exposure or were killed by Indians.

Below is part of a letter Tabitha wrote much later to relatives, describing losing her wagon in a river crossing and being left to struggle on horseback through "mud, rocks and water up to our horses' sides in crossing [a] twelve-mile mountain," which was "strewn with dead cattle, broken wagons, beds, clothing." Having no cattle to attend to, Tabitha set out ahead of the others, provisioned with three slices of bacon and a cupful of tea. She was accompanied by her elderly, feeble brother-in-law ("the Captain"), who soon became sick and delirious. The excerpt describes Tabitha making camp for the night.

"The sun was now setting, the wind was blowing, and the rain was drifting—poor me! I gathered my wagon sheet, flung it over a

(continued)

Once on the river in our two-person craft, Eric and I are shocked when the first few miles go by in 15 minutes. The week before, a few miles on the Green River took us over an hour. This river, wild with snowmelt, is raring to go. It's sunny and warm today, and I queasily imagine the snow at the headwaters liquifying at a rapid rate. The lump in my throat seems to grow larger. "Hey, quit looking so happy," Eric teases. I try to smile. The lump leaps in my throat, then lodges in deeper.

I listen to the rumble of giant rocks tumbling along the river bottom beneath us. My stomach tenses in synchrony with this firm, projecting limb of a tree, and made me a fine tent. I then stripped the Captain's horse, and tied him, then helped up the bewildered old gentleman and introduced him to his new lodgings upon the naked ground . . . expecting he would be a corpse by morning. Pause for a moment and consider my situation—worse than alone; in a strange wilderness; without food, without fire; cold and shivering; wolves fighting and howling all around me; darkness of night forbade the stars to shine upon me; solitary—all was solitary as death, but the same kind Providence that ever has been was watching over me still. I committed my all to Him and felt no fear."

Tabitha and her brother-in-law made it to Oregon. While living temporarily in the home of a minister, Tabitha discovered a picayune—a small coin worth about five cents in the finger of a pair of salvaged gloves. The resourceful woman promptly bought three needles, traded some clothes for buckskin, and set to making gloves. Soon she was able to support herself. From this modest beginning, Tabitha went on to start an orphanage in the settlement of Forest Grove and helped to found the first school chartered in the territory. Today, she is known as "The Mother of Oregon." Tabitha's letter's closing words reveal her justifiable pride in her own fortitude. "Niker hias scocum Tillscum, Close Tumtum," she penned, attempting to transcribe a regional intertribal jargon. She added this translation: "Me very brave woman, good heart."

eerie percussion. Nope, I decide, smiling doesn't feel appropriate.

The shoreline whizzes by, littered with branches and small trees. Mid-river, a 20-foot tree with a root ball the size of a refrigerator floats alongside us. Eric pushes on the oars to slow us down and let the tree pass; if we need to maneuver quickly, we don't want our oars catching in its branches.

For the next 22 miles, evergreens up to 60 feet long float by constantly. Eric turns navigating among these obstacles into a game of "dodge the tree," but I don't want to play. Things feel too unpredictable. The map, I've discovered, is nearly useless with the water at this level. Some of the rapids have washed out, disappearing beneath high water. Other rapids have formed where they normally don't exist. And the river prevents us from going ashore to scout the rapids before running them. It is moving so swiftly as we approach rapids that it flushes us right past possible landing zones.

It takes only two hours to go 25 miles, and we decide to stop for lunch—peanut butter sandwiches, granola bars, and beer. I can't drink. No beer for me—I already feel out of control. As we eat, we decide to camp here. It's not the camp we had planned on, but most camps we've passed are underwater.

We de-rig the boats to set up a common kitchen and our personal tent sites. As I set up our tent and help chop veggies for chili, I study the other people in our group to see if anyone else seems nervous. The guys drink beer and set up horseshoe stakes, seemingly unfazed by the furious river. The two other women, sisters, hang out by the shoreline, heads together in conversation.

I set out alone for a walk. I can't join in the jollity, and I'm tired of pretending I'm not scared. All I can think about is the river; all I can feel is anxiety. As I walk uphill through the trees, away from the social bubble, I wonder why I'm so afraid. I find no answers. The lump gets bigger.

By morning, the river has risen another foot, and the sun shines bright and hot all day. By day three, the river is up several more feet. So far, several other rafts have flipped, but Eric and I have managed to stay right side up. I'm trying to be brave but the dumb lump persists. Usually Eric and I spend our river time laughing, watching for birds, and having water fights. For three days, however, fear has stricken me into uneasy silence. "I want the real you back," Eric complains.

Before running the biggest rapid of the lower Middle Fork, Weber, we stop for lunch at Rattlesnake Creek. I leave the others eating by the boats while I refill my water container with the creek's fast and clear snowmelt. Crouching on the creek bank, I listen as fist-sized rocks roll toward the river, joining the giant boulders. Hot tears pool in my eyes and drop into the icy water. I'm tired of acting brave. My body aches from three days of clenching.

Stop crying, I think. But I can't stop. Small sobs rise, shaking my shoulders. I clench more tightly, squeeze my arms around my legs, but the tears keep coming. Sobs escalate into heaves. And then I stop squeezing, letting the tears flow freely, feeling their shudder begin in my heels and travel through my limbs before reaching my eyes. Again and again, I say, "I'm scared."

Abruptly, the tears stop. I sit on a smooth rock and, for the first time in three days, I feel calm. The same rumbling rocks sound more musical than ominous. I breathe deep, splash my face, find a smile and join the group. I even laugh when they notice I've been crying.

"I just thought I'd add a few more drops to the river," I joke. "But I guess it's big enough already."

After lunch, Eric and I pull down the straps on the cataraft as tight as we can. We have in mind Weber, a rapid with a wicked reputation. Before we get there, we pass several waterfalls—long free-falls of ice-cold water exploding into airborne droplets. The sun-struck spray from Veil Falls mesmerizes me, thrilling me with the beauty of water united with air. I marvel out loud, "So this is why I came here."

Weber is around the corner and, as we approach it, we see the waves, confused and big. Inside me, fear marries excitement, pulsing in my fingertips. There's no tame sneak route we can take to play it safe. In a split second we decide to run center through a haystack of giant cross-waves. Running through Weber, I feel the Middle Fork's true force. There's no thinking, only being. There is wave, there is stroke, there is grunt. Each moment is reaction; each movement is reality. There's no place for fear, only energy.

Once we're through, a new feeling swells in me. Gratitude. A giggle rises in my throat, displacing the lump. "We did it, baby!" I sing to Eric. "Hallelujah!" For the first time this trip, I look downriver with anticipation instead of dread. "Four more days, and I'm so glad to be here with you."

Taking out at Vinegar Creek, 99 miles later, we row our boat right up to our GMC truck in the flooded parking lot. The river, we discover, is running at 96,000 cubic feet per second, the highest recorded flow for June 10. The water level has doubled since we put in. There is sobering news of a death on the river the day before.

As I pose in the water for a final group photo, a wide grin spreads across my face, and I realize that for the first time in over a week, I feel entirely safe. But there's also another feeling: Along with relief at being off the Salmon, I feel pride in the me I've met on this journey—a woman who can admit fear and be strengthened by it. Tears come again, but this time they are tears of thanksgiving, and the lump is gone. I watch as my tears join the waves, and I know that someday I will return.

Rosemerry Wahtola Trommer, who lives in Telluride, Colorado, is the editor of the "Virtue Victorious" volume, Charity, *and the author of two books of poetry,* Lunaria *and* If You Listen: Poetry and Photographs of the San Juan Mountains.

> *"Fire is the test of gold;*
> *adversity, of strong men."*
> —Seneca

SAILOR ALONE IN A WILD SEA
Derek Lundy

The Vendée Globe is a round-the-world solo race in the most dangerous waters on earth, with no stops and no assistance. This account is based on interviews with sailors in that race as well as the author's own sailing experience.

Y ou've slept for exactly an hour and a half, the first sleep in more than a day. One of your earplugs falls out, and the noise suddenly swells. You take out the other plug to listen to the wind and the racket of your boat surfing under a small staysail alone in the Southern Ocean. You swing your feet around the leecloth and carefully stand up, keeping a tight grip on the handrails. The weather is moderating but it's been bad. You consider putting on a survival suit, but the ten-minute struggle out of your salt-stiff foul-weather gear and into the cumbersome suit is more than you can face.

Bracing against the boat's quick roll, you wait for a lull and slide into the gimballed chair at the navigation table.

The radar works, the first time in a week. You count four bergs within the radar's two-mile sweep. There must be ice chunks— growlers—everywhere. The outside temperature is 20 degrees below freezing, with the wind chill. You look through the ports but can't distinguish sea from sky. Solid water sweeps the side-deck every few seconds, blocking your view. Condensation from the cabin top drips onto your head and the chart table.

You are exhausted in spite of your nap. The cut on your left hand has become infected again. You realize it was the pain from the cut that woke you, not the noise.

You piss into your latrine bucket and wedge it carefully behind

the companionway steps. The wind is slackening minute by minute. Soon, you'll have to go on deck and get up more sail. You need some hot food, some porridge and popcorn. You eat it out of pots, shoehorning yourself into the slot that keeps you upright, between the steps and the berth, feet planted, muscles working.

You open the hatch, clip on the harness, roll outside into the cockpit, and slam the hatch shut again. Only a little spray escapes below. It's daylight, visibility about 50 yards. Cold. You can smell the ice. You unfurl half the genoa and hoist the triple-reefed main. The boat surfs in the 30-knot wind. The seas seem bigger than before, evidence of an approaching low.

You watch the boat sail for a few minutes. The albatross is still there, keeping station ten yards off his quarter. You feel you've been on the boat forever, and still the boat's tumultuous rush is exhilarating.

Crawl below to the chart table. There's more ice on radar. You type an e-mail to your main sponsor: Everything is fine, a week to the Horn and then I'll get pissed on champagne. Holding up, no real problems, just that old Southern Ocean funk.

You don't mention the bergs, your saltwater boil, the cut that

COURAGE IS THE PRICE

Courage is the price that Life exacts for granting peace.
The soul that knows it not, knows no release
From little things:
Knows not the livid loneliness of fear,
Nor mountain heights where bitter joy can hear
The sound of wings.

How can Life grant us boon of living, compensate
For dull grey ugliness and pregnant hate
Unless we dare
The Soul's dominion?
Each time we make a choice, we pay
With courage to behold the restless day,
And count it fair.

—Amelia Earhart

Amelia Earhart composed this in 1927, when she was an earthbound social worker who competed in flying meets for fun. The next year it was published in a Survey magazine article by Marion Perkins, her settlement house boss. Earhart achieved many firsts as a female pilot before she and navigator Fred Noonan disappeared in 1939 on a Pacific leg of their attempted round-the-world flight.

EYES WIDE OPEN OR ELSE!

I've got to find some way to keep alert. There's no alternative but death and failure. *No alternative but death and failure,* I keep repeating, using the thought as a whip on my lagging mind; trying to make my senses realize the importance of what I'm saying. I kick rudder over sharply, skid back into position. But there's no use taking it out on the plane; that's unfair; it's not the plane's fault; it's mine. I try running fast on the floorboards with my feet for as many seconds as the *Spirit of St. Louis* will hold to course. Then, I clamp the stick between my knees while I simulate running with my hands. I push first one wing low and then other, to blow fresh air through the cockpit and change pressures on my body. I shake my head until it hurts; rub the muscles of my face to regain feeling. I pull the cotton from my ears, fluff it out, and wad it in again. I must keep glancing at the turn indicator, hold the needle in center with my feet.

"I'll set my mind on the sunrise—think about that—watch the clouds brighten—the hands of the clock—count the minutes till it comes. It will be better when the full light of day has broken. It's always better after the sun comes up. As that dazzling ball of fire climbs into the sky, night's unpaid claims will pass. The desire for sleep will give way to waking habits of the day—that's always happened before And yet, I'm not sure—it's never been like this before—I never wanted so badly to sleep."

—*Charles Lindbergh*

These were the famous aviator's thoughts as he struggled to stay awake during his historic trans-Atlantic flight on May 20, 1927. Lindbergh had been unable to sleep the night before he left New York to solo to Paris. The nonstop flight took 33 hours. His vivid memory of the flight is excerpted from his book, The Spirit of St. Louis.

won't heal. In fact, you're more salt-wet and scared than you ever imagined possible.

Now the genoa is flogging, a noise like a series of explosions. The mast shakes and the hull groans. You crawl back out on deck. The wind is up, to 40 knots or so. The low has arrived sooner than you calculated. It is impossible to furl the genoa; the gear is jammed near the top pin. You strap on your climbing gear and haul yourself up the mast. At almost eighty feet above deck, you reach the snag and free it, one arm and both legs wrapped around the gyrating mast.

Back on deck, shaking, you drag down the mainsail and secure it. Now the wind is roaring at 50 knots, maybe more. Your cut has opened up again, and there is fresh blood on the sail. Back in your berth in soaked oilskins, you realize you've been on deck for two hours.

The low sweeps over, the sustained wind rising to 60, then 65 knots, screaming and wailing round the mast and rigging. The boat begins angling down at 45 degrees or more and snapping back in quick whiplash rolls; it's the feel of a vessel out of control, the autopilot beyond its dumb capacity. You strap yourself into the berth. Nothing to do but hang on and endure the pounding. Water slops around in the aft watertight compartment.

You watch. The dim light fades and the phosphorescent wave crests flash like jewels. A growler thumps and scrapes down the hull. You listen for incoming water and wait for the broach that means the ice has stripped off a rudder.

Nothing. You're lucky again.

Derek Lundy is the author of Godforsaken Sea *(Algonquin Press, 1999), an account of the 1996-1997 Vendée Globe. He lives in Toronto.*

SECTION II

◆ CHAMPIONS ARE MADE ◆ OF THIS

"You become a champion by fighting one more round. When things are tough, you fight one more round."

—JAMES J. CORBETT

WHEN THE GOING GETS TOUGH
Devorah Stone

I walk into the weight gym at Douglas College in Vancouver, a concrete cube with impact mats and free weights. No music. No television. No flashy leotards.

"Hot potato!" shouts a short, muscular woman, tossing an 11-pound ball to the man opposite her as if it is a beach ball. Her eyes appear enormous behind thick, heavy glasses. This is my friend Nancy Carpenter, a Canadian Woman's Master's weightlifting champion. She and the other members of the Boomerangs, a power and weightlifting club, are warming up for their workout.

Approaching a young man Nancy is coaching privately, I ask, "How did you find her?"

Grinning mischievously, he replies, "Tough."

I laugh, but I know it is a good answer.

* * *

Nancy Carpenter was born on an airplane in 1956, spoiling her parents' second honeymoon. Three months premature, she was rushed to a hospital as soon as the plane landed. Medical staff determined that she weighed just three pounds, four ounces and had congenital vision problems. They doubted she would survive.

Nancy did survive. But she always felt different growing up, finding herself a target for teasing. Perhaps it was partly because she was the child of immigrants, Jews from Hungary; or perhaps because she remained small for her age and wore glasses from an early age. Perhaps it was also because she always seemed to be the new kid at school, a result of frequent moves across Canada and the United States as her engineer father shifted from job to job. But nothing attracted other children's cruel comments more than Nancy's love of sports. "Hey, tomboy," they would shout. "Is that baseball glove part of your hand?"

Even her teachers expressed disapproval. "One day, you'll trade in that glove for a wedding ring," she remembers one of them remarking.

This was during the '60s and '70s, when athletic opportunities for girls were limited. But Nancy knew what she liked to do—play the games the boys played. And play she did, finding a place on new teams whenever her family moved, the only girl on almost every team. Despite her short stature and poor eyesight, she could run and slam basketballs in the net and hit baseballs as well as the guys.

When she got teased, she comforted herself with the fantasy of being as strong as her hero, Charles Atlas, the amazing weightlifter she'd seen on TV. No one ever made fun of him.

Nancy did have one faithful supporter, her father. When she was 11, he bought her weights, even painting them a celebratory red. Another time, he turned their spacious backyard into a softball diamond for her, ripping up grass for the carefully measured baselines.

Throughout college and later, working as a high school phys. ed. teacher in Calgary, Nancy—by now at her full height of 5 feet, 2 inches—continued to participate in every sport she could. But eventually her failing eyesight forced her to give up team sports. She was having trouble seeing the net or the goal, or even figuring out who was on her team.

Luckily, weightlifting was opening up to women. In 1995, at the age of 39 and legally blind, Nancy decided that since she had just enough sight to judge her balance, she would compete as a master athlete, the designation for weightlifters over 35.

But first, she needed to find a coach. Good coaches usually concentrate on training potential young champions. Could she find a topnotch coach willing to train an inexperienced older female? She turned to Gary Bratty, a former Canadian weightlifting

> *"The will to win is important, but the will to prepare is vital."*
> —Joe Paterno

champion, but in their first meeting, he seemed determined to discourage her from her quest.

"What makes you think you've got what it takes to be a weightlifter?"

"I'm strong, I've always been strong," Nancy said confidently.

"Weightlifting isn't just about strength. It's also about technique and flexibility."

"I can learn. I'll do whatever it takes."

"Most weightlifters start in their teens. To be any good at all, you'd have to work your tail off, every day of the week."

"I will. I'll even set up a gym in my apartment."

"Then there's my pay. Can you afford it?"

Nancy's deteriorating eyesight had forced her to leave teaching, and she had taken a job as a lab assistant at a biotechnology lab. Bratty's fee would take a big chunk out of her paycheck every month. She'd need to work weekends and subsist on peanut butter sandwiches. "I'll find the money," she replied.

Bratty paused for a suspenseful moment. "OK, you're on," he said, flashing a smile—his first since the interview had begun.

Nancy joined the Boomerangs, the mixed gender and age group of weightlifters coached by Bratty. Weightlifting became her life outside of work, and Bratty and the other club members became her family, cheering her on. After a full day at work and a trip home to eat dinner, she would travel an hour by public transit to the Douglas College gym. After two hours or more of practice, she would head back home, tired and sore. On days when she practiced at home in her mini-gym, she sometimes fell asleep on the bench press, surrounded by the weightlifting posters that plastered her walls.

When Nancy began, she had good strength and speed, but she needed to increase her flexibility and coordination—a difficult task for an older athlete. She concentrated on stretching the small muscles in her shoulders, ankles, and hamstrings, sticking with challenging exercises for weeks or months before seeing improvement. She also began learning the right way to lift a weight, avoiding moves that might injure her body or disqualify her in a competition.

"It's important to be mentally ready, not just physically ready," Bratty repeatedly told her. "See the lift in your mind before you attempt it. See every part of your body in the right position, at every stage of the lift." Nancy learned to visualize herself squatting and grabbing the bar with a firm overhand grip, hands shoulder-width apart. Next she would envision herself raising her hips and knees, lifting the bar to her knees, then lifting the weights to chest level as she moved her arms outward. Step by step in her imagination, she would rehearse the remaining movements until the moment when she jerked the weights overhead. Only after this mental exercise would she be ready to do the actual lift.

Usually an athlete must train for five years before competing; but after only two years, Nancy's coach told her, "You can do it. You've worked as hard as anyone I've ever known, and you're ready to compete."

Nancy entered the provincial championship in British Columbia for her gender, age and weight group, and easily won. She went on to get the silver in the Canadian nationals. Now she was ready for her first international competition, the International World's Masters, held that year in Canada.

Nancy approached that competition with determination, despite the butterflies in her stomach. As she prepared to clean and jerk 57.5 Kg—126.5 lb—she reminded herself of Bratty's words: "See the lift in your mind." Closing her eyes, she walked herself mentally through the steps she knew so well by now, until she felt calm and totally focused. Then she bent down and lifted the weights over her head, feeling power and control in the synchronized movements of her arms, knees, and bottom.

The judges posted their scores. Nancy had broken a world record! As she mounted the podium to accept her gold medal, she thought of her father, now dead, and wished he could have been there to share this moment. All her efforts and sacrifices had been worth it. Like a boomerang, she had come back.

Devorah Stone is a freelance writer who has lived all her life on the Canadian West Coast. Nancy Carpenter still competes as a weightlifter and is completing a Ph.D. in biochemistry.

> *"Just keep going. Everybody gets better if they keep at it."*
> —Ted Williams

MY COACH'S VOICE
Morgan Barth

Looking back on my four years of high school wrestling, I freely admit that I wasn't a natural at the sport. Rolling around on a sweaty mat was never my idea of a good time, and many days I was tempted to head down to the locker room, shower off for the last time and never look back. But I stuck with it—and learned lessons about tackling life that will stay with me forever.

I went out for wrestling as a freshman, drawn by the chance to be around a bunch of tough-looking seniors who impressed me with their camaraderie. It would be cool to be on a team, and besides, it looked like a good way to get my flabby body into shape. There were, after all, a lot of cute girls in the ninth grade.

In that first year I got a lot of what I wanted from wrestling: I belonged to a team; I got to slap five with upperclassmen in the cafeteria; I increased the size of my biceps; and I got my own varsity warm-up jacket. Perhaps I even impressed a girl or two. But the price I paid was two hours of torture every day after school.

Coach McKee began every practice by having us run countless tight laps in the gym, followed by several hundred sit-ups, 50 push-ups, and calisthenics. After the sit-ups, I felt like throwing up; and I never could do all 50 push-ups.

The agony continued as Coach drilled us in simple moves like double-leg takedowns and wrist chops. As I was thrown to the mat repeatedly during takedown drills, I was sure I could feel my internal organs being jolted out of place. To make things worse, I couldn't seem to get any of the moves right. With each clumsy attempt I made, I came to expect Coach McKee's bellowed correction: "Keep focused, Barth!" "Head up, elbows in and SHOOT and drive!"

After the first few weeks, I began to look for ways to avoid Coach's scrutiny during drills, picking a practice spot out of his line of vision. Behind Coach's back, I was a pushover: Falling over like a sack of potatoes hurt much less than fighting a take-down. But despite my best efforts at slacking off, I still had hardly enough energy to walk to the water fountain by our half-time break.

The last part of practice inflicted a new round of cruelty on my weak body: Laps around the gym while carrying a teammate pig-gyback; wheelbarrowing—trotting on my now-collapsing arms while a fellow wrestler held onto my legs like handles; and wind sprints—which actually did make me throw up more than once. Dragging myself home one evening, I found solace in the thought that at least I had it easier than those World War II soldiers forced on death marches through the Bataan jungle. Thank God, wrestling season would soon be over.

Sophomore year, I quashed my misgivings and returned to wrestling. It still made me feel important to walk down the school halls in that warm-up jacket, with the tiger mascot emblazoned on the left front and my name in curly script on the right. But the biggest reason I returned was my fear of losing the respect of my coach and teammates if I quit. It was a funny thing about Coach McKee. Although he spent half the time yelling at us, the other half he spent praising us. "I respect you just for sticking with this sport," he would sometimes say, and I would feel a surge of pride. And so every day after school, I found myself tan-gled again in half-nelsons and headlocks, envying my more care-free friends and loathing the sport that took over my life from November through February.

That second season, I still tried to get away with as little work as possible—although even those halfhearted efforts nearly killed me. Some days, however, team captain Dave Tchlockian—

as tough as his name sounds—would grab my arm and say in his deep jock voice: "You're drilling with me, Barth." Boy, did he make me work!

When it was time for live wrestling, I'd look around for a freshman partner, but frequently, Tchlockian would intone, "Don't even think about it. You're still with me, Barth." I couldn't wait for the water break—or even a slight injury—to give me a brief reprieve from the mat.

The summer after tenth grade, I had a lowly office-boy job at an ad agency in downtown Manhattan. I spent my days collating photocopies and running errands through the hot, humid city. To beat the boredom, I daydreamed. And nearly every time I daydreamed, my mind drifted back to wrestling. If it makes me miserable, why don't I just quit? I asked myself this almost daily. I resented the sport invading my thoughts even during the summer, when I should have been carefree.

That summer I was 16, and in the evenings I had lots of fun with my friends at Mets games and concerts in the park. But even in the midst of these activities, there were idle moments when the sport wrestled its way into my mind. Why? I asked myself. Why did this sport exert such power over me? Was it the power of hatred?

Then it came to me. It was not wrestling that I hated. Yes, practice hurt sometimes. But I had gained much strength and mental stamina. And nothing in my lazy summer had given me half the feeling of accomplishment I experienced after an intense practice match against Tchlockian. What I really hated, I realized, was my own halfhearted effort, my lack of commitment to doing my best. Coach McKee had said it many times: "You get out of wrestling exactly what you put in." And I was not putting in enough. The choice for the fall became clear: I would have to work harder in that gym and try to tap into the power of my sport.

November came, and I went back to the gym with a new attitude and a new openness to Coach's wisdom. I was trying harder, so he didn't yell so much. But often, when he saw me wind up on my back, he would tap his temple with his forefinger, reminding me of the power of the mind. Daily, in a husky Long Island accent, he repeated his mantra: "Where the head goes, the body will follow." When yelled across the mat, this sounds like simple physical logic. But now I really understood that this was a message about the mental challenges of wrestling: Focus, discipline, and commitment. I found that when I put my best effort into practices, mentally as well as physically, those last few drills—though not exactly easier—were not the torture they had been. With more effort, more grit, I could rise above the exhaustion and pain.

We lost a lot of meets that year. Yet the most positive memory I carry with me is of a moment in the middle of defeat. We had just been creamed by the opposing team, and were gathered for Coach's post-game critique. I kept my head down, waiting for him to rip into us. Instead, he said, "I'm proud of you all. We may have lost out there, but every one of you pushed himself to his limit. Sometimes it's not about winning, but about getting better for yourself. You're only a loser when you give up. And you guys didn't give up."

Nothing is greater than having the referee hold up your hand in victory at the end of a hard-fought match. That did not happen to me often, not even during senior year, when I was captain of the team. But as silly as it may sound, I still felt like a winner, because I had learned that wrestling is about persevering, and bettering yourself, and being responsible for who you are, even when you do lose.

It has been more than two years since I was on the wrestling team, but whenever I feel frustrated, something in my psyche brings me back to the mat, and I know that I must focus more clearly. When things slip from my grasp—as did so many of my opponents—I remind myself that I must give my all, whatever the outcome. When I need a jolt of motivation, I still hear Coach McKee's bark, encouraging me to do better.

I heard it last summer, high up on Rolling Mountain in Colorado. My hiking partner and I were trying desperately to reach the saddle of the mountain before a lightning storm hit, so we would not have to turn around and cut short our backpacking trip. Rain soaked my chilled, exhausted body, and I could feel the blisters on my feet pulsing in pain as I struggled up the steep slope under the weight of a heavy pack. I might have turned back if not for Coach McKee's voice, telling me not to give up. But we made it to the 13,000-foot crest and descended into the protected valley below.

It is not just during adventurous moments that I hear Coach's voice. It kept me at the stove when I ached to walk away from a summer job cooking in the steamy kitchen of a Mexican restaurant. It prods me to stay awake until the early hours of the morning to finish a history paper. It steadies me during a maddening conversation with an upset girlfriend. And now when I hear that voice, I wonder if it is no longer Coach McKee's, but my own.

Morgan Barth is a student at Williams College in Massachusetts.

THE POWER WITHIN ME
Maria Portgee

My first day at Georgia State University, in 1989, I noticed a table set up to recruit new members for the rowing team. I also noticed the two burly guys at the table and the photos on display—all of other burly guys rowing. Girls obviously did not row at this school. I dismissed the fleeting notion of trying a new sport.

I didn't think about rowing again until my junior year when my friend, Gail, approached me. There'd been a change of leadership on the rowing team, and months earlier she'd been asked to join. Now she was the captain. Only five feet tall, she didn't actually row; as coxswain, she faced the rowers and steered the boat. In contrast, I am five feet nine, and a solid 175 pounds. "Come on, girl," she begged me, "help me out here. We need some more women on the team. Almost everyone else I've talked to is afraid of getting sweaty or breaking a nail."

I decided to do it. It would be great exercise—and maybe I'd meet some of those burly guys.

As African-American women in a sport dominated by white males, Gail and I attracted our share of stares. "You row?" people would ask disbelievingly when they saw my team jacket. Others asked, "How did you get involved in such a white sport?" "What are you trying to prove?" Such remarks left me feeling hurt and resentful. But I also pitied the people whose minds were so tightly closed.

No one on the team made a big deal about the color of my skin. We had more compelling concerns, such as improving our form and power. We had no coach, so we taught ourselves by trial and error, with the assistance of training manuals and videotapes. Our school was 45 minutes away from our boathouse, so practices were sporadic. We would meet early in the morning, after class, whenever we could get enough crewmembers together to fill a boat. When other teams learned we didn't have a coach or a regular practice schedule, they expected very little from us. But because we were in charge of our own training, practices were a "want to," not a "have to," and we put our whole hearts into them.

That summer our team signed up to compete in the statewide Georgia Games, with our women's four-seat boat entered in the novice category. This would be my first competition, and I was determined to do my best, although the heat and humidity of Georgia in July turned every practice into an endurance test. The stagnant, steamy air inside the un-air-conditioned boathouse made warm-ups on the rowing machine especially torturous. But I practiced faithfully, and each week the odometer on the rowing machine showed my time improving.

An encouraging moment was the first time my performance on the machine surpassed that of a male teammate; I felt like Superwoman! I was careful not to gloat out loud. But inside, a voice roared exultantly, I *beat a guy. I beat a guy!* That small victory kept me going as I prepared for the Games. I gave my all in each practice, no matter how high the humidity, no matter how sore I might be the following day. Yes, I was a woman on the crew team, and yes, I was one of the only black people out there—and proud of it!

As the date for the Games drew nearer, my feelings of strength began to give way to doubt. How would our four-woman boat fare against teams that had the benefit of coaching? "Just stop worrying and do it," I told myself. But my stage fright grew.

The day of the competition was hot as usual. At the lake outside Atlanta where we were to row, it was 95 degrees in the shade—and there was no shade. People from rowing clubs and schools all over Georgia thronged the beach. Gail and I joined our teammates and parents in the bleachers to watch the races before ours. We tried to enjoy ourselves but I could tell that everyone, including me, was terrified.

Our men's boat of four started first. The rest of us stood at the dock and cheered them on to a bronze medal. Although I was very happy for them, my stomach knotted tighter and tighter. As each passing minute brought us closer to my boat's race, my mind began to spin out of control: *If I fake a leg cramp, I won't have to go out there. I can't do this! We're so awful; we won't even make it to the finish line!*

Finally our time came. We climbed in our boat and made our way to the starting line. As soon as we reached it, I realized I had a problem. I had been drinking bottle after bottle of water to combat the heat, and my bladder was about to burst. I quickly resolved to use my discomfort as motivation. The faster I rowed, the faster I could get to the bathroom. I have never been more on edge than I was at that moment.

At the sound of the pistol, we shot off the starting line. "Go! Go!" Gail yelled at us, calling for power strokes, which take every ounce of energy. All I could feel was speed; all I could hear was Gail's voice; and all I could see were the other boats falling farther and farther behind us. I was actually doing this. We were actually doing this. We were far ahead of the other boats. We were really good!

I should have known things were going too well. We were halfway to the finish line when I "caught a crab." Placing the blade of the oar in the water at an angle instead of perpendicular with the water, I lost control of it, and it ended up in front of me—not where it should be. The entire team had to stop while I struggled to place my oar in the correct position.

Suddenly drained and weak, I fought unsuccessfully to pull the oar into place. I could see the other boats getting closer and closer. Then—in an instant it seemed—they had passed us. *Please God, help me*, I pleaded. *We're going to lose and all because of me.*

Then it happened: I got the oar back into position. But would it be too late? We would all have to recapture the energy we'd had when we were so many boat lengths in front of the others. Gail started shouting at the top of her lungs, drowning out any other sounds. "Power twenty! GO GO GO!!" I could not see where the other teams were. I couldn't tell if they had already finished the race. I only knew I had to give everything I had.

Then Gail announced the impossible: "We're gaining on them! Faster! Faster!" I was relieved to learn that the other boats had not yet reached the finish line. "Give me a power twenty and you can catch them," Gail bawled. At that moment nothing else mattered—not the heat, not my need for a toilet, not the ignorant comments some had lobbed my way. I just gave each stroke all the power I had.

Gradually I could see the tips of the sterns of the other boats on either side of me. "Another power twenty," Gail cried. With each powerful stroke, I could see, one by one, the members of the other teams. We were passing them all. Pulling, pulling, pulling, we left them farther and farther behind. Gail began to scream, "We're in first place! We're in first place!" This made me pull even harder. My only thought was that I refused to let my team and myself down.

The energy within me kept building and building. Then it was over, and Gail began cheering and clapping. As for me, all I could do for a while was put my face in my lap and gasp for breath. I felt dizzy, delirious and nauseated, yet I was happy and ready to accept my gold medal. But first I made a stop at the ladies' room.

The next day the results of the race were printed in the *Atlanta Journal and Constitution.* I cut out the announcement of our victory and put it in my wallet. Now whenever I feel bad, I take that clipping out. And as I look at it, I remember: Nothing is impossible.

Maria Portgee lives in Atlanta, Georgia, where she works for the US Disabled Athletes Fund, a nonprofit organization that introduces the disabled to competitive sport opportunities. Her music reviews have been published in the on-line magazine Black Rebel Digits.

> *"Push yourself again and again.*
> *Don't give an inch*
> *until the final buzzer rings."*
> —Larry Bird

THE RECEIVER WHO REFUSED TO QUIT
Bruce Nash and Allan Zullo

Lehigh University senior Rich Clark made the most amazing play of his collegiate football career when he caught a game-winning touchdown pass against Dartmouth.

What made the catch so sensational was that Clark caught the ball with two broken hands!

In fact, the tough wide receiver from Tunkhannock, Pennsylvania, played two games with broken bones in both hands, refusing to quit despite terrible pain.

Throughout the 1991 season, the 5-foot, 10-inch, 180-pound Clark was one of the top receivers for the Lehigh Engineers. But no one really knew how much heart and determination Clark had until the second game of the season, when the Engineers played the University of Connecticut.

By the end of the third quarter, Clark had made seven catches—including two for touchdowns. But early in the final period, he was knocked out of bounds after making another clutch reception. While he was sprawled on the ground, his left hand accidentally was stepped on by another player. Clark winced in pain and then ran over to the bench, where team trainer, Jack Foley, taped the hand. "I think you'd better come out," Foley told the player. "This doesn't look very good."

Clark shook his head and said, "No, it'll be OK. I can still play." Before Foley could say another word, Clark dashed back onto the field. Despite his wrapped hand, he caught two more passes, giving him ten receptions for 117 yards in the game, which Lehigh won 35-19.

The following day, X-rays revealed a fractured bone near Clark's left wrist. Although his hand was put in a cast and it was painful to play, he continued to practice. When the trainer sug-

gested that Clark sit out the next game, the player told him flatly, "No way! I'm playing. I've still got one good hand."

But the very next Saturday, early in the game against Columbia, Clark suffered an almost identical injury—this time to his other hand. Clark caught a pass over the middle. But as he tried to pull the ball into his chest, a pair of defensive backs crashed into him, and his right hand was caught between their helmets.

After the play, Clark trotted to the sideline in terrible pain as he held his rapidly swelling hand. "I hurt this hand, too," he told Foley.

"Now for sure you'll have to stay out of the game," said the trainer.

"No way," Clark replied. "Fix me up. Then I'm going back in."

After getting his right hand wrapped, Clark played the rest of the game, catching seven passes for 120 yards to lead Lehigh to a 22-9 victory over Columbia.

However after the contest, Clark discovered that his right hand was broken. When he showed up for practice on Monday, he was wearing a cast on each hand.

"Look, Rich," said Coach Hank Small. "I know how badly you want to play against Dartmouth next week, but a receiver isn't much use without his hands. How are you going to catch the ball?"

"I don't know, Coach," replied Clark. "But I'll figure out a way. Just give me a chance."

Clark worked hard all week in practice relearning how to catch passes without his hands. Over and over, he practiced cradling the ball with his arms and body instead of grabbing the pass with his hands. At the same time, Clark had to learn how to block all over again. "You can't chuck the defenders with your hands anymore," warned the coach. "You've got to learn to block with your whole body instead of just your hands."

Every day that week, long after his teammates had headed for the showers, Clark remained on the practice field, forcing himself to learn new ways of catching and blocking without using his hands.

The following Saturday, at Lehigh's first home game of the season, emotions were running high. The Engineers were hoping to extend their unbeaten streak to four games. Most of all, they wanted to avenge their loss to the Dartmouth Big Green the year before.

Wearing the two clumsy hand casts, Clark started the game, determined to show that he could still help his team. But in the first quarter, he dropped the only two passes thrown to him. From then on, the pass plays sent in by the coach went to the other receivers. Clark continued to block and run his pass routes, hoping that his number would be called again.

Late in the game, the Engineers trailed Dartmouth 28-23 when they mounted a last-ditch drive. Lehigh marched from its 20-yard line to the Big Green's 15 with less than four minutes left.

Coach Small then sent in a play that surprised everyone in the huddle—70 Pass Smash Delay. It called for Clark to delay a second at the line of scrimmage before cutting sharply across the middle. The play—Clark's favorite pass route—would challenge the heart of the Dartmouth secondary.

In the huddle, quarterback Glenn Kempa grinned at Clark. They had practiced the pass play endlessly. Both knew that by calling the play, Coach Small was showing he had faith in Clark's ability to make the catch despite his injured hands.

"This one's for you, buddy," Kempa told Clark, his roommate and best friend. "Let's get it done!"

At the line of scrimmage, Kempa barked out the signals. Clark took off on his route and cut to the middle at the four-yard line just as Kempa threw the pass. Clark leaped and cradled the ball softly against his chest and held on. When the receiver came down, a Dartmouth defender was already hanging on his back, but Clark stayed on his feet and lunged toward the goal line.

Clark then was hit by a second defender. But as he was going down, Clark reached out as far as he could. Holding the ball between his two broken hands, Clark stretched just far enough to place the pigskin over the goal line.

It took the officials a few seconds to untangle the players, as Lehigh fans held their breath. Then the referee's arms shot up with the signal. Touchdown! Lehigh kicked the extra point and held on in the final minutes to win, 30-28.

Along the sidelines, Clark's happy teammates pounded him on the back. Coach Small looked Clark in the eye and said, "I knew you could do it, Rich. Way to go. I'm proud of you."

Proving he could play with two broken hands, Clark caught eight passes for 141 yards the following week, as Lehigh beat Northeastern University 35-22.

The casts came off two weeks later, and Clark finished his collegiate career with 155 receptions—good for second place on Lehigh's all-time receiver list.

Bruce Nash and Allan Zullo have collaborated on several books. Nash is a Los Angeles-based TV producer; Zullo, who lives in Ashville, N.C., recently published The Nanas and the Papas: A Guide to Grandparenting.

FARTHER! FASTER! LONGER!

L egend has it that when the Greeks defeated the Persians in 490 B.C., a messenger was speeded from the battlefield at Marathon to announce the victory to the leaders of Athens. Reaching his destination, the runner gasped out, "Rejoice! We conquer." Then he collapsed and died.

The first modern Olympic games, in 1896, set the marathon at 24.8 miles, the supposed distance of that famous run. That contest was won by a Greek shepherd, Spiridon Louis, in 2 hours, 58 minutes and 50 seconds. Today the standard marathon is 26 miles, 385 yards, and the world record is held by Khalid Khannouci of Morocco who, on October 24, 1999, ran the distance in 2:05:42. That's over a mile farther than Spiridon and almost an hour faster. The holder of the women's world record is Tegla Loroupe of Kenya, with a time of 2:20:43.

Ultramarathons, races far longer than the marathon, are gaining popularity. The longest certified race is a 3,100-mile competition sponsored by the Sri Chinmoy Marathon Team, run on a half-mile loop in New York. The hero of ultradistance running is Yiannis Kouros, a Greek Australian, with many remarkable accomplishments to his credit. For instance, in November 1984, Kouros ran 1,000 miles in 136 hours and 17 minutes–under six full days. In 1997, during a 24-hour period, he ran the equivalent of more than seven consecutive marathons, averaging an incredible 3 hours and 21 minutes per marathon.

Marathon dance contests were popular during the Depression, with couples competing to stay awake and remain in motion long enough to win a cash prize. The initial 20-minute rest periods were progressively decreased and eventually eliminated during the course of the contests. The rules required that dance steps be at least ten inches wide and that eyes not be closed for more than 15 seconds at a time. According to the *Guinness Book of World Records*, the all-time marathon dance champs were Mike Ritof and Edith Goudreaux, who, on August 29, 1930, entered a contest in Chicago and lasted over 214 days.

The New York to Paris Automobile Race of 1908 surely qualifies as a marathon. One chilly February morning, six competing teams set out from

New York City in their canvas-topped cars, intending to reach France by heading west across the United States and proceeding through Alaska, the frozen Bering Strait, Siberia, Russia, Poland, and Germany. The journey was almost 20,000 miles long and driving conditions were primitive; contestants spent almost as much time digging themselves out of the snow as they did in their cars. The winner, an American mechanic named George Schuster, finally wheeled into Paris on July 30—and was immediately pulled over by a gendarme for driving without a headlight.

The only limit to the types of marathon activities appears to be human imagination. Consider these accomplishments of stamina and determination.

•In September 1998, 36-year-old Pat Farmer spent 24 hours running up and down an 87-floor skyscraper in Sydney, Australia, covering a total of 101,934 stairs.

•During a 70-day period in 1969, Tom McClean rowed a boat 6.1m long from Newfoundland to Ireland.

•And then there is the 1998 deed of Benoit Lecomte, who *swam* the Atlantic in 72 days!

•Finally, there's the July, 2000 mountain marathon feat of Ricky Denesik, who climbed all 55 of Colorado's 14,000 feet plus peaks in slightly over 12 days.

MAGIC PABLO
Mark Brazaitis

P ablo and I liked to play "Let's imagine." We'd be walking down the street, one of us with a basketball cradled under his arm. Clouds would be gathering in the east, as they tended to do in early evening. A light rain—*chipi-chipi* is what everyone in town called it—might even be falling.

"Let's imagine," Pablo would say, "that Michael Jordan is walking with us."

He would smile. "What would these people say?" he would ask, pointing to the women in dark blue *cortes* and white *huipiles*, the native dress in this town in the northern mountains of Guatemala. "What would they do?"

"They'd be amazed," I'd say. "They wouldn't know what to do."

Pablo would agree. "They'd probably run. But we'd just keep walking down the street, the three of us, to the basketball court."

Pablo was 16 when I met him, another indistinguishable face in my English class of 45 students. I was 25, newly arrived as a Peace Corps Volunteer in Santa Cruz Verapaz, a Guatemalan town of 4,000 people.

The night after my very first English class, Pablo knocked on my door. I invited him in and he entered, looking around shyly. On a table in my dining room, he saw a copy of *Sports Illustrated* that my stepfather had sent from home. He pointed to the cover photo.

"Robert Parish," he said. "The Chief."

Pablo, it turned out, knew as much about basketball and the NBA as I did, and I was a former sportswriter. I don't know where he got his information in this remote rural town. But somehow he knew not just Robert Parish and other All-Stars, but obscure players like Chris Dudley and Jerome Kersey—and could talk about them like an NBA beat reporter.

Pablo would come to my house at night and we would draft imaginary line-ups. Pablo liked non-American players. Hakeem Olajuwon was his favorite. He liked Mark Aguirre because he'd heard that Aguirre's father was born in Mexico. Dikembe Mutombo, Manute Bol, Drazen Petrovic—selecting our imaginary teams, he'd always draft these players first.

I didn't get it. Why would he pick Vlade Divac instead of Charles Barkley? But the longer I lived in Guatemala, the better I understood.

The American presence in Guatemala is about as subtle as a Shaquille O'Neal slam dunk. Pepsi covers entire storefronts with its logo. In Santa Cruz, the town basketball court is painted with a Coca-Cola motif, right down to the backboards. In remote villages, children wear "Ninja Turtles" shirts.

Little of America's affluence has filtered down to Guatemala, however. Pablo's family, although better off than most in town, cooked with firewood and had no indoor plumbing. Pablo's mother sold lunches in the market to supplement what her husband made as a foreman in the government's local road-building department.

Pablo and I had long arguments about who was the best player in the NBA: Hakeem Olajuwon versus Michael Jordan. Hakeem versus Patrick Ewing. Hakeem versus Magic Johnson.

Pablo stuck by his man.

Pablo and I played basketball on the court next to the cow pasture. Pablo was 5 foot 5 inches. I am 6 foot,1 inch. When we first began playing, I could move him around with my body, backing him close to the basket. If I missed, I was tall enough to get the rebound. In games to twenty-one, I would beat him by nine, 11, 13 points. But Pablo never seemed discouraged by my easy victories; good-naturedly, he would dismiss them as luck and vow revenge.

Pablo's dream was to dunk a basketball. We calculated how many feet he would need to jump—about four.

Pablo drew up a training plan. He would jump rope two hours a day to build his leg strength. Every other day, Pablo would ask his younger brother to crouch, and he would leap over him, back and forth, for half an hour.

Weeks later, Pablo came to my house and asked me to set up a hurdle in my courtyard. I stacked two chairs on top of each other, then another two chairs a few feet away. I placed a broom across the top chairs and measured: The broom was four feet off the ground.

"I'm going to jump it," Pablo said.

"You sure?" I asked him.

"Yes, I'm sure."

We stood there, gazing at the broom.

"You sure?" I asked.

"I'm sure."

More gazing.

Then he backed up, took a few quick steps, and jumped. His knees shot into his chest. He leapt over the broom like a frog.

"You did it!" I yelled.

"I can dunk now," he said, grinning.

The next morning, we went to the basketball court. Pablo dribbled from half court and leapt. The ball clanked off the rim. He tried it again. Same result.

"I don't understand," he said.

I didn't have the heart to admit I'd misled him: To dunk, he'd have to jump four feet without bending his knees.

As a player, though, Pablo was getting better. He couldn't dunk, but he'd learned to use his quickness to drive by me and score. He had grown stronger. I could not back into him as easily.

Also, he had developed a jump shot.

Despite his interest in basketball, Pablo's best sport was soccer. Pablo was known as a good playmaker. Quick dribbler. Not a scorer, but a good passer. Soccer's equivalent of a point-guard, not a power forward. I'd seen several of Pablo's games and had watched him make gorgeous, sky-touching passes.

My last week in Guatemala as a Peace Corps Volunteer, I attended a game Pablo played in. The game was tied 1-1 going into the final minutes. Pablo's team had a corner kick. The crowd, about a thousand strong, was silent.

The ball soared into the air. A mass of players, including Pablo, gathered to receive it. Pablo jumped, his body shooting up like a rocket off a launcher. His timing was perfect. His head met the ball, and the ball flew past the goalie, into the net for the winning goal.

Pablo's teammates paraded him around the field on their shoulders. People from the crowd, per custom, handed him money.

When I talked to him later, I didn't need to point out why he'd been able to jump that high. He said it himself: "It's basketball. I learned that from basketball. From trying to dunk."

Pablo had learned many things, and our last face-off at the hoop, the evening before I left Guatemala, ended in a tie. As we walked back to my house, a light rain—a *chipi-chipi*—fell.

"Let's imagine," Pablo said, "that you and I played against Michael Jordan. Who would win?"

"Jordan," I said

"No," Pablo said. "We would. Believe me, we would."

Mark Brazaitis served as a Peace Corps Volunteer and Technical Trainer in Guatemala from 1991 to 1993 and 1995 to 1996. He won the 1998 Iowa Short Fiction Award, and is the author of The River of Lost Voices: Stories from Guatemala *and of the recent novel,* Steal My Heart *(Van Neste Books).*

THE LAST DAYS OF 'FIREPLUG'
Rusty Fischer

I used to play football when I was little. Actually, I was never really little. I was one of those boys the clothing manufacturers euphemistically refer to as "husky." In fact, I was so pudgy that I got to play football a whole year ahead of my friends. In the Florida beach town where I grew up, the Mighty Mites football league had a weight requirement instead of an age limit. If you were heavy enough, you got to play. And by the age of eight, I was heavy enough.

The only problem was that by the time I turned 11, I was too heavy. When you weighed more than a certain amount, they made you stop. And that was fine with me. Three half-year stints of daily football practice and games all day Saturday had been enough. I'd stayed on as long as I had to prove that I wasn't a quitter. But I would have been happier sitting at home reading a book.

However, Dad was one of the team's big sponsors and best friends with the coach. He loved stopping by practice every day to watch me play. And on game days, when I'd make a big tackle or a great block and he'd hear his son's name over the loudspeaker, he was like a kid at Christmas. I'd felt that if I quit, I wouldn't just be letting myself down, but my father as well.

So in I'd gone. Day after day. Week after week. Year after year. Until I was 11 and weighed over 200 pounds.

I thought that would be the end of it, once and for all. And, in a way, it was.

To make sure each player was under the official weight limit, the referees lugged an old-fashioned doctor's scale around with them. The heaviest kids had to weigh in before each game. If the scale tipped past 200, off went the player's cleats. Then the helmet and the shoulder pads. Sometimes the jersey and the pants, or even the undershirt and the socks! Coach knew I was in trouble the day I had to step out of my underwear to make weight.

So he came up with a bright idea. The very next Monday at practice he presented me with a shirt made out of a black garbage bag. "Put it on," he grunted, pointing out the ragged holes for my head and arms. "Start running around the practice field, and don't stop until I say so."

I began running, the only kid on the field. On the sidelines, my friends sat on their helmets, interrupting their talk about the latest *Mad* magazine or *Star Wars* movie to snicker and point at me. After every lap, I'd wave questioningly at Coach.

"Keep going, Fireplug," he'd grunt around the mushy cigar in his mouth.

Fireplug was my nickname; I figured it had something to do with my shape.

Every day I had to run in that stupid garbage bag, sweating off weight. I'd hear it crinkling beneath my underarms, the sound drowning out my ragged breathing as I stumbled through the weeds, lap after lap. If I tripped and fell, as I often did, the other players would laugh—but not as loud as Coach. The only one who didn't laugh at me was my dad. Although it must have embarrassed him to see his chubby son running around the field in a garbage bag, he showed up at practice every day to cheer me on.

Unfortunately, the garbage-bag shirt did not achieve dramatic-enough results. So Coach arranged for me to use the sauna at a local high-rise condominium. I rode my bike there the next Saturday, and Coach handed me my black plastic garment, ushering me into a cedar-lined closet with two benches and a red metal shelf full of glowing hot rocks. He poured water on the rocks to build up steam, and then shut the door on me with a sardonic smile.

Outside the porthole window, I could see him chomping on glazed doughnuts and sipping coffee. My stomach roared. As usual on game day, I had foregone breakfast, and I would not be allowed to eat again until after weigh-in, when I would be too weak to do anything but sit and pant. Only then would Coach shove me full of candy bars from the concession stand, to give me the energy to play ball again.

As I sat in the sauna, hungry and swimming in sweat, I had time to think. I'd been trying to lose weight for over a year. I had frequently skipped breakfast; I had brought bag lunches to school, filled with unappetizing low-calorie foods; I had even tried to make myself throw up. But nothing seemed to work. Now here I was starving and sweating at eight on a Saturday morning, while the rest of the team feasted on Frosted Flakes and watched cartoons. They were still in their pajamas, while I was here in a garbage bag. Why?

I clearly realized that not only had I been knocking myself out for something I didn't want to do, *I didn't have to do it any more.*

Then I remembered Dad. I pictured him getting ready for today's game, pulling on his size XL team shirt and filling a big red thermos with Gatorade for me. For three long years our football seasons had been his favorite time of the year. It was our special time together, just he and I. Thoughts of disappointing my father and of no longer having special time with him made my empty stomach hurt even more.

Still, I couldn't take the sweatbox and all the rest of it any longer. There must be other special things my dad and I could do together. He would understand my decision. Wouldn't he?

Who knows, maybe he'd freak out and yell and scream. The thought of it almost sapped my resolve. But I firmed up my mind. I could live with Dad being angry for a while. It'd be hard, but if I could live on carrot sticks and Melba toast for a whole year, I could surely walk on eggshells at home for a few months!

My heart fluttered and my stomach flip-flopped, but I finally stood up on wobbly legs and walked out of the sauna.

"Did I say you could get out of there?" Coach bellowed when he returned from the pool deck a few minutes later and found me enjoying one of his doughnuts.

I shook my head, but Coach was waiting for an answer. "I quit," I said in a shaky voice.

"You quit?" he fairly laughed, looming over me. "You can't quit. What would your Dad think? Don't you want him to be proud of you any more?"

But that was just it. If my Dad couldn't be proud of me for just being me, then what was the point? I was a good kid. I stayed out of trouble, got good grades, and made him a Father's Day card every year. Did I have to torture myself, too? Did I have to earn our special time together? Wasn't that kind of stuff supposed to be free?

I told Coach again it was over. That was when he called my father. After explaining the situation, Coach grunted and handed me the phone. My hands were shaking, and I was glad I wasn't doing this face to face.

"Son," my dad said quietly, "is what Coach said true?"

"Yes," I whispered into the phone.

"You don't want to play football any more?" he asked simply.

If I was going to do this, I was going to do it right. "I never did," I gasped.

Dad's laughter surprised me. "Then why did you go through all those shenanigans?" he asked. "I thought you wanted to be the next Joe Namath!"

I hung up the phone and headed for my bike, feeling as if I'd just lost ten pounds! Coach stood there fuming as I pedaled away.

> *"Perserverance is not a long race; it is many short races one after another."*
> —Walter Elliot

Although I quit football for good that year, I do have Coach to thank for two things: I learned that I could stand up for myself; and I took up jogging, something that I've stuck with ever since. In fact, running in freedom, I learned to love the solitude of a simple morning, feeling the sweat on my skin, the breeze in my face, and the in and out of my breathing as I loped leisurely about my small beach town. With increased self-respect and fitness, I started carrying myself differently. And gradually people stopped calling me Fireplug.

I remember the last time I heard that nickname I'd hated. My family and I were waiting for a table in a local restaurant when Coach sauntered in on his way to the bar. He greeted my dad rather coolly and then eyed me with open disdain. "What's the word, Fireplug?" he asked.

Dad looked at me for an instant, then turned firmly to my old trainer: "You mean Rusty, right, Coach?"

Coach's response, grumbled around the cigar in his mouth, was inaudible, but it didn't matter. Our table was ready, and Dad kept his hand on my shoulder the whole way there.

Rusty Fischer resides in Orlando, Florida, where he is a writer/editor for a small publishing company.

SECTION III

◆FACING ILLNESS AND INJURY◆

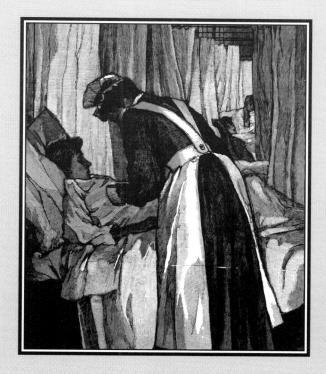

*"God will not look you over for medals,
degrees or diplomas but for scars."*

—ELBERT HUBBARD

LIVING WITHOUT A CURE
Cecilia Maida

When I was 19, happily employed and full of plans for a career and family, I awoke one day with a piercing pain in my abdomen. After a hospital stay and numerous tests, the doctor told me dispassionately, "You have PKD, polycystic kidney disease, a fatal condition. You were born with it—and at 19, you've already outlived your prognosis." He hesitated, then added, "You'll be lucky to live to 30."

I froze. I suddenly seemed disconnected from my body and, as if from a great distance, I heard the doctor explain that there was no cure or treatment for the disease. All that science could offer was medication for the pain that would soon overwhelm me, from cysts that would rupture and eventually enlarge my kidneys to the size of footballs. "You will probably never work again," the doctor warned. "And don't even think of having children. This disease is hereditary."

That day, I wished I were already dead. How could I live—in pain, all my dreams gone, with the time bomb of PKD ticking away? Seeking comfort, I headed to my friend Clyde's house at the beach. As I sat sobbing in his living room, I heard a swoosh, swoosh from the street. "My friend's here," Clyde said. I looked out the window and saw a woman on a skateboard. But this was not your typical skateboarder: Clyde's friend had no legs, and only elbow-length stumps where arms should have been. Transfixed, I watched her efforts as she used her stumps to hoist first her skateboard and then herself up each of the stairs outside Clyde's house. Once inside, she used her skateboard as a step onto a low coffee table, flung herself backward from the table onto the couch, and struggled into a seated position. She was clearly exhausted, but she threw her hair back and beamed the brightest, happiest smile I had ever seen.

Looking at her, I thought, *If she can smile, how can I sit here crying? My problems are nothing compared to hers.* I believed she had been sent to me, to make me see all the things I still had despite my disease.

I made up my mind that I would not passively wait for death. I moved from Houston, Texas, to beautiful California. Determined to support myself, I forced myself to work as much as possible. "God," I would pray most mornings, awaking in pain, "I'm going to get up, but I need your help." When I had to dress for an office job, even my clothes aggravated my misery. My panty hose might be loose in the morning, but I knew that as the day progressed and my abdomen swelled, they would cut into me unforgivingly. *Wish I could ask my boss if I could dress casual,* I would think—but I believed that if I told management the reason for my request, I'd be replaced by someone healthy.

Remaining seated creates pain for me, so by the time I reached the office in my car I was often in tears. Once at work, however, I pasted a smile on my face, fearing that someone might discover I was sick. When stationary tasks such as typing or xeroxing increased my pain, I would practice one of my pain management techniques. For instance, I might focus all my attention on the details of Monet's water lilies in the print opposite my desk, imagining that I was redirecting the pain impulses from my brain into its pastel depths. As a last resort, I would sneak a portion of a pain pill, fearful that if I took a whole one, I would slur my words. I was always proud that my employers, while unhappy about the number of days I missed, stated that when I was present, I was the best employee they had.

When I was well enough to work, I made sure that I played, too. Despite the pain, I tried everything—snow skiing, guiding river rafts, kayaking, riding motorcycles, skateboarding, bungee jumping, and water skiing. Fearless, I would take a pain pill and go for it! *Drowning in a kayak accident will make for a much more exciting obituary than death by kidney disease*, I thought. It was my way of getting the best of my illness. As a bonus, the adrenaline rush from taking physical risks would temporarily override my body's focus on pain.

Although I was determined to make the most of whatever life remained to me, I often felt alone and hopeless. One of my big frustrations was the attitude of the medical profession. Because many people with this ailment do not experience pain, most doctors dismissed my complaints that I hurt. "It's all in your head," one suggested. "Patient appears to be making up pain in order to get disability," wrote another in his notes.

My 30th birthday came and went. I had outlived my deadline for death, and it seemed I had a number of years ahead of me. The following year, 1991, I made a discovery that was to change my life.

I had phoned the Kidney Foundation, to check whether they knew of any new research on PKD. "Hold, please, and I'll give you the number of the Polycystic Kidney Research Foundation," said the woman on the other end of the line. I felt faint from shock. Over the years, I had rarely found anyone who had even heard of PKD. Now I could be part of a network of fellow sufferers and knowledgeable doctors and researchers. I wasn't alone any more!

The Foundation's meetings became part of my therapy. There I learned that PKD is the most common life-threatening genetic disease in the world. I particularly remember one conference in 1996. I had gotten a cup of water and seated myself for the keynote speech. "We are honored," said the master of ceremonies, "to have as our speaker today Dr. Steinman, from Harvard University, who will talk to us about PKD and pain." PKD and pain! I almost choked on my sip of water. I listened intently to Dr. Steinman's speech. During the question-and-answer session afterward, I raised my hand and stated, "I have been in pain from PKD for 17 years. Do you have any success stories to share about people improving?"

"First, let me tell you that your pain is real," he responded. "Many doctors, myself included, have been guilty of denying pain like yours because we didn't know how to fix it. All I can say to you is, stay strong, because we are working to find a cure." Tears streamed down my face as I left the room. A medical researcher believed I was in pain. Dr. Steinman might not have a cure for my physical pain, but he had helped heal the pain in my heart.

Toward the end of 1996, my pain grew so bad that I could no longer work. I began receiving Social Security and could feel myself giving in to despair. I dreaded waking up each day to face life with no job, little money, and no accomplishments to feel proud of. *I wish I had the guts to end it all,* I often thought.

But one night, sitting glumly on the couch, I remembered the woman on the skateboard, that first day I had found out I had PKD. I thought of how much comfort I'd given and gotten through my Foundation connections. I also thought of my old travel dreams. I'd never seen most of the places I'd yearned to visit before I heard my diagnosis, because I had always used my vacation time as sick days. That night I made the biggest decision of my life: I would see the United States. In the spring of 1997, I used a lump-sum payment from Social Security to buy a used 26-foot Coachmen recreational vehicle, stored the possessions I didn't need and began the ultimate road trip. I set off to visit friends across the country and to go to Washington, D.C., to lobby for more funding of PKD research; I wanted to try to raise public awareness of my disease and offer my support to as many ill, suffering people as I could. I wanted to inspire others, just as the woman on the skateboard had inspired me.

Since I began traveling in my motor home, I have explored 29 states and have formed warm friendships with strangers in little towns and teeming cities. I drive on good days, when I don't have to take strong painkillers, and stay a month or so at each destination. I tell everyone I meet about PKD. I am always elated when I hear from people with PKD who have never heard of the Polycystic Kidney Research Foundation.

One memorable incident occurred when I was visiting Texas and ran into Mike, a childhood friend. We talked for a long time, and I mentioned the conference I was planning to attend on my kidney disease. "What kidney disease?" he asked. When I told him, he fell silent, then blurted out, "My entire family has PKD—and with the pains I've been getting in my back, I'm afraid I'm getting it too." After the two of us got over our shock, I learned that neither Mike nor anyone else in his family knew about the Foundation. Although Mike's revelation saddened me, it made me feel good to make him aware of a new resource.

"Don't give up hope," I urged him. "You're not alone, and scientists are working to find a cure." That's where I get my strength—from encouraging others.

On bad days, I rest. But even when pain and fatigue attempt to get the best of me, I force myself to get up, reminding myself that there are 12.5 million people with polycystic kidney disease out there who need help. To energize myself on those days, I may look at a tape of my television spots or check my e-mail and find a message from someone with PKD asking me for advice. I live by the motto, "God's gift to you is life, and what you do with your life is your gift to Him."

Cecilia Maida suggests that those interested in learning more about polycystic kidney disease contact the Polycystic Kidney Research Foundation at 800-PKD-CURE.

THREE STRIKES BUT SHE WAS *NOT* OUT
Geraldine Mellon

O ne o'clock, two o'clock, three o'clock, rock . . ."

"Mary Chambers," as this valiant woman will be called here, and her three children were speeding through the Indiana countryside. It was a drizzly summer day in 1989, but their raucous singing to '50s tapes dispelled the gloom of the weather.

The children, Bobby, 9, Jessica, 8, and Elaine, 7, looked forward to visiting their father's farm. But if Mary had her way, there would be no visits with John, her ex. Eight years earlier, with a baby on each hip and pregnant with a third, she had decided she could no longer tolerate his philandering and his towering rages. Mary still remembered John's final taunt, "You'll never make it without me!"

Just watch me, she had thought. *God knows I've been through worse.*

Mary had done well enough to buy a cheery little house in a suburb outside Chicago. Her job as a registered nurse with the Veterans Administration was a killer, but her salary was good.

Stopped at a traffic light and thinking of lunch, Mary glanced into the rearview mirror: A car had roared over the hill and was aiming straight for her bumper. She eased the Camry forward, but it was not enough. There was the terrifying crunch of metal striking metal, and Mary's car and three others went flying into the intersection, where they landed joined and jointed like a Chinese dragon. Bobby's screams filled the crushed Camry. Within minutes, EMS attendants lifted him into an ambulance. Mary, the quiet, efficient nurse, had already run her gentle hands over Bobby's body. Mary, the mother, whispered, "Thank you, God, it's only a muscle spasm."

As she collected Bobby from the emergency room, Mary was vaguely aware of a creepy sensation in her neck. By nightfall, the sensation had escalated into excruciating pain, the calling card, Mary would eventually learn, of a cracked vertebra in her neck.

A worn, green, flowered couch soon came to know every contour of Mary's body. For months, it was the one place she could sleep. In the morning, Mary gingerly eased her way upright from the depths of the couch, joint by joint, trying to protect her neck. She felt beads of sweat forming on her upper lip from the effort and drew in her breath. *Dear God, help me through this day.* She unbuttoned her gown, let it slip to the floor, then moved with tentative steps toward a scarred straight-back chair, piled high with her clothing. Electrical jolts raced down her leg with every step. As she reached for a tee shirt, jolts shot through her arm.

Finally clothed, she shuffled in slow motion to the kitchen. *Thank you, God. Let's make the coffee.*

The children fed, somehow, and off to school, Mary shambled to the den, half-heartedly searching for the giant rubber bands provided by her physical therapist. "Morning, noon, and night, if you can," the therapist had advised. "Let's try to strengthen those back and shoulder muscles, get the lower body back in alignment." Sighing, Mary hooked a red band over the back of a wooden chair. Holding onto the chair, she hoisted her trembling right foot six inches, placed it in the band, lowered it to the floor. *Oh, God, that hurts, that hurts!* Gritting her teeth, she began another stretch. *I survived childhood, I survived my marriage, I'll survive this.*

***

Aunt Susan's words drifted through her mind. "Just a baby in a high chair. Your father unbuckled his belt, and your eyes filled with tears. I never felt so sorry in my life. Beating a baby over a bite of food! Why, you couldn't even walk or talk!"

There had been love in Mary's mother, but not strength enough to rescue herself and Mary from her husband's brutal belt. "I want to leave," her mother had often wailed, "but he'll kill me."

Early on, Mary swore she would not be a victim like her mother. When she was eight, a news reporter on the TV offered a piece of information that would sustain her throughout the rest of her childhood. "In California, at age 18, a person is an adult, legally of age." *I live in California!* she thought elatedly. *I can leave home when I'm 18!*

About that time, a Baptist Sunday school taught Mary about God. She was skeptical at first but one day, trembling at the sound of her father's angry voice, she whispered, "God, please help me." Soothing warmth spread through her body—"a kind of hug from God," she remembers. From then on, Mary talked with God often.

***

"Let's try a shot of cortisone on that neck," suggested Mary's physical therapist. "The exercises aren't working." But the night after the shot, familiar jolts raced down Mary's arm. *Scratch cortisone off the list,* she thought. *Well, God, nothing's left. I'll talk to the surgeon.*

Six months after the accident, a bone sliver from Mary's hip was successfully fused to her damaged vertebra, eliminating the pain in her neck. The morning of her discharge, however, she was puzzled. *How irritating! I can barely understand a word that nurse says. Why is she babbling?*

The children were in Indiana again, and back at home Mary turned on the TV for company. Though it was hours before sundown, the room grew eerily dark. Mary whirled into the void, her body thudding heavily to the carpet, where she lay until the morning sunlight coaxed her to consciousness. She pushed herself upright and wobbled into the bathroom. *Dear God, is that me?* The right side of the face in the mirror was heading south.

"No cause for alarm," the surgeon said when he checked her out later that day. "It's just a little stroke, a transient ischemic attack, TIA for short. Damage is temporary; it'll be gone in a few hours."

But within a week, Mary was so quickly forgetting words she read that she couldn't comprehend even the shortest sentence in the newspaper. Her gait became stiff-legged and sidling, like a crab. She couldn't recall everyday words. "Bobby, please turn off . . ." she might begin, staring blankly at the kitchen sink. *What do you call that stuff coming out of the pipe into the sink?* Shaking her head weakly, Mary would have to get her message across by pointing to the running water.

As Mary's functioning deteriorated, it was apparent that this was no TIA, but a major stroke. The doctor had no answers. "We don't know why stroke sometimes follows surgery, Mrs. Chambers, but it does. In your case, it could be from the accident. We just don't know."

Somehow the children managed much of the housework and laundry. But Mary still cooked meals: Social Services had ruled that they could send someone in to cook for her, but not for the children, so Mary had declined their help.

Shopping for groceries was an ordeal. Hanging on to the grocery cart for support, Mary dragged herself back and forth through the supermarket like a dazed alien, unable to remember where to find the items on her list. *Let's see, I need creamer. Oh, it's back with the coffee, in the aisle I was in ten minutes ago!* At the checkout counter, she would hand the cashier her money—all of it—explaining, "I've had a stroke, and I'm having trouble counting."

The most frightening incident was when Mary almost set the house on fire: She asked herself, *What is that awful smell?* Then it hit her—she'd left chicken frying on the stove. Moving from the living room to the kitchen at the pace of a frantic snail, she grabbed the smoking skillet, just shy of ignition, and dropped it in the sink. From then on, a trusty little timer ticked away in Mary's hand if she dared leave the kitchen while cooking.

Mary set about relearning her lost skills as best she could on her own. Lack of transportation and child care made outside rehabilitation impossible. Hunched over the yellow Formica kitchen table, she clutched a pen in her uncooperative, stroke-weakened right hand. It could take her 15 minutes to scratch out: "Dear Jane, How are you? I am . . ."

Day after weary day, Mary struggled to relearn math: *Two times four is . . . eight. Two times five is . . . ten. I'm getting it! Oh, God, I'm getting it . . .*

Scrolling recipe ingredients on TV cooking shows served as flash cards. Gradually, written words began to stick together with meaning. Six months into her self-designed rehab program, Mary cuddled in the depths of the faithful green couch, and opened a book of poems by Emily Dickinson, an old favorite. She read and understood the opening lines!

The first Day's Night had come—
And grateful that a thing
So terrible had been endured.

Mary's ears throbbed with the drum of her heart. She carefully closed the book, as her memory gave the final line.

I told my Soul to sing.

Two years passed and Mary continued to progress. Forced into medical retirement, she moved to a home in the country on the outskirts of a small college community in Kentucky. It is a modest frame house, missing paint here and there, but looking out on acres dotted with grazing goats. Rabbits nibble daintily. A rooster struts his stuff. "Can you tell the kids and I love animals?" Mary asks me with a grin. She points to the lopsided chicken coop. "I built the coops myself," she says proudly. "Of course it took me three months to do what an able-bodied man could do in one day."

Ten years after the accident, Mary sips early-morning hot coffee at her kitchen table. The fused neck moves only with the shoulders. The crab walk is gone, but her movement, like her speech, is measured and deliberate. About her losses, Mary is philosophical. "Strange as it sounds, the accident and stroke were a gift," she muses. "Without them, I would still be slaving away at a grueling job. We make it okay on my retirement."

A couple of college texts lie on a nearby chair. Mary is a Fine Arts major at the local college. "In high school, I really wanted to go into art, but I had to escape and earn a living. So I chose nursing instead. Now I can follow my heart."

Mary Chambers checks her list-of-the-day, a vital ritual with her unreliable memory. A rooster crows, celebrating the dawn light. Mary pauses to pray: "Thank you, dear God, for the blessings of my life. Thank you, dear God, for peace."

Gerry Mellon is a friend of the woman called "Mary Chambers" in this essay. Ms. Mellon's work has appeared in Equus, The Western Horse, *and* Trail Tails. *She and her husband live in west Kentucky.*

MEDITATION ON A DOG BITE
Daniel Asa Rose

My lawyers have instructed me not to say, "I was bitten by a dog." They much prefer, "I was attacked by a rottweiler." Pithier, they feel, more slam dunk. But if they're adamant on that point, they're even stricter about what else they don't want me to say: "And I'm a better man for it."

They feel, not unreasonably, that such a declaration ruins my case. They would rather I talk about how getting mauled by a 140-pound beast during a summer evening's jog was no picnic, about what a drag it was spending a night in the E.R. being given intravenous antibiotics, about how dismaying it is for me to keep seeing the scars on both my biceps. They want me to recount how six months ago I didn't know what rottweilers were, and how they now dominate my dreams, hulking brown-black mini-bears, like Dobermans with heft. They like me to point out that on a recent safari in Zimbabwe, I didn't mind lions sniffing at my tent at night; it was rottweilers growling behind a chain link fence in airport security that got me sweating.

And no question about it, I can talk about these things, for they are true: It was terrifying; I was traumatized; dog attacks are grisly events. But as usual the lawyers are missing the point. Getting bit was also distinctly empowering—a middle-age milestone.

For starters, I was amazed at how different this attack was from the one I suffered when I was a boy. In the middle of this one, I had enough wits about me to think, "This is a dog attack and that's all it is." When I was 12, and roughly the same size as my assailant, dog was all I could think: dog fur in my eyes, dog roar in my ears, dog teeth in my calves. I was toppled, engulfed, inundated by dogness.

This attack couldn't have been more different. This one left room for awareness of road, lawn furniture, sunset-dappled cloud behind a particularly majestic pine tree. This one was, oh hell, don't let my new Reeboks get slimed. As I felt the layers of my skin crack and give way to his fangs, there was much more to the moment than the mere insult of muscle yielding to canine dentition. There were clear slow-motion questions: "Hmm, has he had a rabies shot?" "Are the owners covered?" Even the philo-karmic question: "Isn't it better that I take this hit than a child or a 120-pound woman?"

And it got better from there. I mean, forget Jack Nicholson in *Wolf.* Since the attack I star in my own private movie called *Rott,* wherein I find myself taking on the attributes of a rottweiler. Suddenly, as I flash back to the way his jaw locked, I find I am more doggedly determined with the phone company when they charge me for a 900 call I know I didn't make. Suddenly, as I flash to his bulk, I rationalize that I am putting on "girth" as opposed to "fat" when I reach for a second helping of frozen yogurt. Plainly, the rottweiler has become what the Jungians would call my power animal. And what's interesting to me is how my power animal is different from what it would have been in my earlier days. In my teens and 20s I saw myself as a fox or a roost-er. Now, in my middle-aged tenacity, in my hound-like hereness, I feel like a rott. Despite being the one bitten and not the biter, I feel like those primitive men who ate the hearts of their foes to absorb their souls. *Ich bin ein rottweiler.*

In the afterglow of the attack, I recognize that I am braver now than I was in my 20s and 30s. Partly, I admit, this is because now that I'm in my mid-40s, I have less to live for. The number of women I've loved and sons I've reared and books I've pub-lished are not enough, in any category, but are at least sufficient to make me feel, if my head was in the jaws of a wild animal and I was being shaken till my neck broke, that I wouldn't be obliged to yelp: "Wait, I haven't yet begun to live!"

But also my greater bravery is due to the confidence that comes with seniority. When you've dived with sharks, hopped freight with outlaws, and dated a girlfriend like my last, it takes more to rattle you. You're more likely to look at a set of snarling teeth up close and say, "Knock it off, nitwit. I've been here longer than you."

It all comes down, I suppose, to grit. One has more of it at 45 than when one's a pup. But it's also a different kind of bravery— less the kind that desires to bring a ballpark to its feet and more the kind that wants to nurture things along. More and more I eschew the violence we were taught to think was virile, to find that hysterical now, as I admire the more manly quality of forbearance. As a consequence, I find I can afford to be kind to my second wife in ways I couldn't with my first. I can be gentle with flowers; sometimes I don't even want to tread on grass lest I bruise the protoplasm that has lived here long before me and will live here long after. And if a dragonfly lands on my wrist while I'm weeding, I'm happy to let him stay and share. As the rottweiler may have noticed, I'm not so territorial about my body. There's more than enough room for all of us.

So yes, I have been attacked by a rottweiler. But, with all due respect to the legal profession, I endorse the experience wholeheartedly. I now know that, as we grow older, our masculinity can sweeten as it deepens. Were it not for the rottweiler, I might never have had a clue.

Daniel Asa Rose is an O. Henry Prize-winning short story writer who lives in Massachusetts. His new book, Hiding Places *(Simon & Schuster), chronicles a trip he took with his young sons to retrace his mother's family's escape from the Holocaust. This essay is adapted from a story that appeared in the Nov. 1997 issue of GQ.*

ANNIE'S PARTING SHOTS
Sandy Merritt

I met Annie on the tennis courts of a racquet club, set near towering pines in the northern Arizona mountains where I live. She weighed all of 100 pounds and stood five-foot-four, with a wiry, tanned body. At age 64, she hustled around the tennis court, picking up overheads and smashing balls back against her opponents with a fervor that amazed me. Off the court, she was full of cheer and gusto, with a quick smile and warm hug for everyone.

We were the same height but separated by ten years and 50 pounds. Watching us play, it would be difficult to tell that I was the younger. When she invited me to be her doubles partner, I gladly accepted, although I feared that next to her I looked like a Sumo wrestler stuck in mud. Our comradeship on the courts developed into a friendship based on mutual respect and enjoyment of activities, such as hiking, volunteer work and taking classes together.

One night while we were out to dinner with our spouses at our favorite Italian restaurant, Annie's husband, Gene, revealed that she was a survivor of colon cancer. Stunned, I listened raptly as he related how Annie had been diagnosed one day and had undergone surgery the very next. When he finished talking, Annie smiled brightly and said, "Thank God, that's behind us. The doctors said they got it all. Now we can enjoy life." I was relieved to hear that the cancer was old news, nothing to concern myself over.

After we'd known each other for about six months, the club championship came up, bringing with it a memorable chance for Annie to demonstrate her mettle. She and I had agreed that we'd team up again. As the favorites, we'd been excused from the first

round, and after a grueling second-round match, we had advanced to the finals.

The temperature had climbed from the 90s into well over a hundred. Already tired from our marathon match the day before, we slogged onto the court. Today we faced the toughest local team. We looked at them and then at each other and wondered silently if we would be a match for them. Linda, a heavyset woman, had a serve like a shooting star, so fast you wondered if you'd actually seen it; her tall partner, Joan, was lethal at the net. Not our top choice to play today.

"It's a hot one," Linda said, taking a long swig of ice water. "If you guys want to, we could play this on another day."

With my back toward Linda and Joan, I winked at Annie.

"Today is just fine with me," Annie said. "How about you, Sandy?"

"Fine with me."

"Are you guys sure?" Linda asked. "You know it's a hundred degrees already." She took off her red neckerchief, soaked it in a Styrofoam cup filled with ice water, and tied it back around her neck.

"We know," Annie said, picking up the can of high-altitude Penn balls. She popped the lid. "I'll spin for serve." She spun her racquet around on the cement and waited for it to land. "Up or down?"

"Up," said Linda.

"It's down," said Annie. "We'll receive."

"Let the games begin," I whispered.

We'd only had to play two matches. Our opponents had played three. We ran them around unmercifully. The temperature soared. By the end of the second set everyone except Annie looked two steps away from sunstroke.

We split sets. Our opponents won the first, six-four; we won the second one, seven-six. We'd suffered for an hour and a half in the blistering sun, and now faced a decisive third set.

"How about we finish this tomorrow?" Joan offered, her face red, her clothing soaked with perspiration. She gulped water and wiped her forehead with the icy kerchief.

"No. We finish today. I have commitments tomorrow," Annie said, looking at me fiercely. "Okay with you, Sandy?"

Could I say no? I was exhausted. The elevation and the heat had taken their toll. "Great. Let's do it," I answered, more gamely than I felt.

We headed back out to the courts. The bottoms of my feet burned, my head pounded, warning me that I needed to make sure I drank plenty of water. There was a ringing in my ears, like a distant echo.

Barely moving, I halfheartedly hit balls. Annie ran around and covered for me. She never let up in that third set, running, hitting, pounding the ball at our exhausted opponents. Time after time, she called out energetically, "I've got it!"

Of course, we won in the third set. I have the plaque hanging on my wall to prove it. We shook our opponents' hands and said all the right things: "Tough match. Thought we wouldn't make it. You guys played great."

When they left, our husbands came over and gave us the congratulatory hugs we so richly deserved. Annie turned to her husband and asked in a tone of voice that betrayed no sign of fatigue, "What time is square dancing tonight?"

About a week later, Annie called me with an alarming announcement. "I saw my chiropractor yesterday. He says he felt a lump in my stomach. We're leaving for California in the morning. I just wanted to say goodbye."

So upset I could hardly speak, I weakly replied, "Good luck. Hope it goes well for you."

When Annie returned a couple of weeks later, she had worse news: "The cancer is back. They can't operate."

"Oh, no," I said, not wanting to believe it. We hugged in silent sadness.

"The worst part is the doctor told me I have to do chemo."

I knew from our discussion that night in the restaurant that Annie hated the thought. "I'm sorry," I said. "I know that's not what you wanted to hear."

Annie began chemotherapy. She would show up to play tennis after that, but she could hardly make it through a set. She looked tired and drawn and unhealthily thin. One day while we were out playing, she said, "I'm not going to do chemo any more. I'm down to 90 pounds, I'm tired all the time, and my immune system is a wreck. This is no life. I'll battle this thing as long as I'm still breathing, but I have to do it my way. There's a place in California that does alternative medicine, and I'm going to try it."

HE BORE THEIR AFFLICTION

To begin is nothing. The hard thing is to persevere." This was written by Father Damien in 1873 as he embarked on the new mission of ministering to exiled lepers on the Hawaiian island, Molokai. At that time, leprosy—or Hansen's disease as it is now called—was untreatable and subjected its victims to a slow, painful death, as muscles, membranes, bones, organs, and nerves degenerated. The lepers sent to Molokai by the Hawaiian king were imprisoned by natural barriers: Sea on two sides and a lava cliff, 1600 feet high, that cut their peninsula off from the rest of the island.

The setting boasted natural beauty but the Belgian priest saw a hellish scene when he arrived. The 700 inhabitants of the colony were living in squalid conditions, with inadequate food and water and no sanitation. Despairing and in pain, the majority dissolutely stayed drunk on an alcoholic brew made from the roots of the ti plant, and they frequently brawled. Many had become so callous, they ignored the piteous pleas of fellow lepers who could no longer move about. Those who died might be tossed into ravines to be scavenged by wild hogs.

After getting acquainted with his challenging new flock, the energetic Damien—who was also a skilled carpenter and builder— threw himself into improving their lot. He badgered the indifferent Board of Health in Honolulu into sending him tools and construction materials. His first project included fencing in a graveyard and building coffins, that respect for lepers in death might be restored.

Damien was naturally daunted by the physical condition of the afflicted. Those in advanced stages of the illness were covered with

"Are you sure?"

"I'm sure."

Annie spent two weeks at a clinic outside San Diego, learning about the plan. Checking in by phone with her husband, I heard about all the changes the program was making in their lives. No more going out to eat, only organic fruits and vegetables, no tumors and oozing, gangrenous sores, and many had lost noses, fingers, hands, arms, toes or legs. The smell of their rotting flesh could be overwhelming. "Many a time," Damien wrote, "in fulfilling my priestly duties at the lepers' homes, I have been obliged not only to close my nostrils, but to remain outside to breathe fresh air."

In time, however, the priest overcame his fear of physical contact with the lepers, for he could not reach the hearts of these people if he treated them as untouchables. Risking infection, he began sharing their meals, embracing them, placing the sacramental host on their tongues, and cleaning their wounds.

Damien spent 16 years in the community, enlisting the more able-bodied to help him build over 375 structures—tidy white cottages with well-tended gardens, and other buildings ranging from a school to a general store. The priest also oversaw construction of a docking facility and a road between the lepers' two villages. He organized a band and community celebrations.

One day in 1884, the priest was soaking his feet, which were aching from the day's labors. Suddenly he noticed that they were red and blistered. He touched his thumb to the water his feet had been resting in and quickly jerked it away, for the water was scalding. He had contracted leprosy; the insensitivity in his feet was a sure sign.

In April 1889, Father Damien died at the age of 49. His story inspired a global campaign to find a cure for leprosy, as well as a flood of contributions to the residents of Molokai. But Father Damien, himself, had given them the greatest gift: the gift of human dignity.

meats except lamb and buffalo, everything cooked from scratch.

About a month later, I saw her. She looked chipper and happy, albeit thin.

"You look great," I said. "Seems like you're thriving on this alternative method."

"It's wonderful. They've put me on an organic diet, taught me new eating habits. Only problem is I can't have my usual cocktail before dinner—and no desserts! But look at me. I've put on five pounds. And I can play tennis again."

Annie returned to the court, perhaps with less energy, but still banging away at the ball. If there were days she didn't feel her best, she never let on. Then one day, after about a year, she didn't show up.

"Where's Annie?" I asked a mutual friend.

"Gene's taking her place," she replied. "He said she's tired today."

When Annie's husband arrived, I cross-examined him. "What's happening? Is Annie okay? Is she going to keep on playing?"

Noncommittally he said, "We'll see."

Nothing trivial could keep Annie from tennis, so I knew that something must be seriously wrong. When I telephoned her, Gene would tell me she was sleeping. She never came out on the courts again. Within two weeks she was dead.

I saw Gene before the funeral, and he told me the story of Annie's final spirited moments. "Just before she died, she sat up on the table in the emergency room, all doped up on pain pills. She flailed those small arms of hers like she was swinging her racquet. 'I got it,' she kept saying, swinging away. 'Got that one. Got it.'" Gene paused, his eyes filling with tears. "She did what she loved up until the end."

Annie Skidmore was a fighter and I miss her.

Sandy Merritt is a former newspaper reporter who now writes fiction in northern Arizona. She hopes to soon find a publisher for her novel, Blackout.

ONE DAY AT A TIME
Bill Asenjo

I t was a cool spring night in Texas. A Marlboro haze settled over the tiny kitchen, barely concealing the odor of pork chop grease. Dirty dishes filled the sink. Occasionally a beer can popped.

Three other men and I sat around an ancient Formica table. Neighbors in a sad apartment building, we met nightly to drink, play poker, and complain about how little our unemployment and welfare checks bought these days. Like the others, I had drunk away my last job. I had come to Dallas from New York City, hoping for a fresh start. But I'd brought my bad habits with me. At age 36, my life was still a mess.

"This straight's gonna get me some Heineken," I boasted, studying my cards. But the beer would have to wait.

Approaching swiftly, like a summer storm, a black cloud bullied its way into the corner of my left eye, and suddenly everything went dark. I was blind.

"Whaa . . ." I started to exclaim. But before the words were out, I slumped over the table like a puppet with its strings cut, paralyzed.

"Call 911!" someone shouted.

***

"You have a brain tumor," the neurosurgeon at the emergency room announced somberly after he examined my brain scan. "A bit larger than a golf ball. We'll operate first thing tomorrow." Surely, I thought, he was not speaking to me. I wanted desperately to be somewhere else.

Anywhere else.

As the horror of my situation sank in, I realized I had no one to lean on. I had distanced myself from my family, both emo-

> *"People are like stained glass windows; they sparkle and shine when the sun is out. But when darkness sets in, their true beauty is revealed only if there is a light within."*
>
> —Elizabeth Kübler Ross

tionally and geographically; I had no friends other than drinking buddies; and I believed I had no God.

As a child I'd been a top student, Boy Scout, and altar boy. But when my grandfather died of cancer, I had felt betrayed. What use had it been to pray for his recovery? What use had it been to be a good kid?

Feeling abandoned by God, I'd stopped going to church, stopped praying, and had gravitated to the streets of New York, finding comfort in alcohol and drugs. They continued to comfort me—or at least numb me—in adulthood, as I drifted from place to place and girlfriend to girlfriend, working sporadically as a bartender, truck driver, and construction laborer. Ashamed of the way I'd let my family down, I'd rarely contacted them, and I was sure they'd written me off. Now, awaiting surgery, I felt hopeless, afraid, and utterly alone.

***

The next morning, surgeons removed part of my skull and began probing, and found that the tumor's tentacles snaked deep into my brain.

Removing it all required six operations, over a period of five months.

Throughout the first long month, I remained paralyzed, drooling, my speech slurred. At times I was in such pain that I would have welcomed death. Surgery restored some of my vision, but my surroundings appeared to me as out-of-focus snapshots taken in dim light. Indignant at the surgical intrusions, my brain short-circuited, causing my body to convulse, like a damaged wind-up toy. Brooding bitterly, I was convinced my life was over.

Despite my pessimism, I was on a slow road to recovery. As autumn replaced summer, I left my bed for a wheelchair. A few weeks later I was able to move about with a cane. "Won't be long before we'll be letting you go," a nurse remarked.

My family surprised me by crossing six states to visit me while I was in the hospital, so when I was discharged, I headed for my parents' home in Florida. But I was back to my old routine and arrived stoned on pain medication and beer.

"Billy, you need help," my father said. "If you want to stay with us, you'll have to go through a drug rehab program first."

I had tried everything from treatment programs to self-help groups in the past—and had failed. But somehow I believed that this might be my last chance. "Okay Dad," I responded, "I'll give it another shot."

I soon found that the no-nonsense counselors at the treatment center wouldn't indulge my self-pity. The first morning there, I joined other patients for group therapy. After sharing how unfairly life had treated me, I waited expectantly for the others to express their concern. Instead, the counselor leading the group leaned forward and calmly said, "Bill, sympathy is in the dictionary between shit and syphilis." Then he casually turned his attention to the others, asking, "Anybody want to talk instead of whine?"

In time, the counselors at the program tough-loved me into acknowledging that I was using my disabilities as an excuse to drink and drug. The build-up of dangerous medications slowly leached from my body. Free of street drugs, alcohol, and painkillers, I began to perceive the world with new clarity. It was as if I'd emerged from a darkened movie theater into the midday sun. Thoughts, memories, and regrets rushed into my consciousness, like bubbles to the surface of a Coke.

One realization in particular gnawed at me: My secure stay at the rehab center would soon end. Then what would I do? I was physically handicapped, emotionally immature; I had no skills or education; and I was scared stiff. I'd always dealt with fear one way: by getting high. Reluctantly facing the fact that I needed more support, I began attending the Alcoholics Anonymous and Narcotics Anonymous meetings offered at the center.

As discharge day approached, I mumbled my first sincere prayer in decades: "If there is a God, please help me."

Once released, I moved in with my parents and continued attending AA 12-Step meetings.

As my health improved, my sister offered me sage advice. "Billy," she said, "you're a disabled college dropout with nothing to offer an employer. I doubt if they'd hire you to flip burgers." She paused, impressed by my bleak prospects. "You'd better register for a class at the junior college."

The idea was daunting. Wasn't I too damaged? My vision was still poor in one eye, and my balance, though improved, was still wobbly. Wasn't I too old? The other students would be 20 years younger than I. I'd been out of school since the Nixon era. Had I forgotten how to study?

Over coffee one morning I confided my fears to a 12-Step friend. "You know," I said, "I'm 38. If I shoot for a bachelor's degree, I'll be 42 by the time I graduate."

My friend looked up from his coffee. "Bill, if you don't die," he said, "you'll be 42 someday anyway. Why not be a 42-year-old college grad?"

And so, almost a year after my last surgery, I joined the registration line at the local junior college, trying to ignore my sweaty palms and the tension in my gut.

Free of mind-changing chemicals, I fell in love with learning. Listening to a lecture on the ancient Greeks, I thought, I heard this stuff almost 20 years ago and thought it was a bore. But without a hangover, it's fascinating. As I studied and applied myself, my anxieties melted away, and I ended the first semester with straight A's.

Even though things were working out, I was still plagued by bouts of self-pity and the temptation to drink and do drugs. And I didn't know how to change that.

At 12-Step meetings, most people reminded me of myself— always rehashing the same old complaints. But there were a few who stood out. They had a sense of peace and purpose, and I longed to be like them. There's a saying in AA: "If you want what we have, do what we do." I noticed that the people I admired were typically involved in helping others. I was ready to "do what they did."

One of these people was a man who was especially active in helping others who were trying to stop drinking. "Why don't you come with me next time I answer calls from AA's hotline?" he asked. I accepted, and we visited people desperate to stop drinking, some of them suicidal, others violent, many simply depressed and broken.

"This hotline work is a two-way street," my AA friend remarked. "You help someone, and it helps you stay sober. There's nothing like it to remind you of how nasty your life used to be."

Following his example, I started volunteering to handle hotline calls, and discovered my friend knew what he was talking about. Finally realizing how fortunate I was not to be drinking, I lost all desire to drink. I also began to experience an unfamiliar emotion: gratitude.

Soon I volunteered to read to a blind man. The first time we met, I arrived in a crabby mood, irritated that I had had to interrupt my busy schedule and fight a traffic jam. But as I read Bernie his mail, it hit me: Bernie didn't have to worry about traffic or rude drivers; he couldn't drive. I settled down to appreciate the simple gift of seeing well enough to read.

I found that the more I helped others, the less I worried about myself and the better I felt. As an unexpected bonus, my volunteer activities were helping me qualify for scholarships. During my second year in school, while completing a scholarship application, I was struck by the difference between the positive, productive person I was describing on paper and the Bill Asenjo who had spent enough time in bars and pool halls to finish several degrees.

Surely I couldn't take much credit for the change, or I would have done it years before. "Whoever or whatever I'm talking to, thank you," I mumbled.

It is a prayer I have repeated countless times over the 13 years since then. For I believe that fateful events are God's way of operating anonymously. And I remain convinced that having a brain tumor was the best thing that ever happened to me.

Bill Asenjo lives in Iowa City, Iowa and is completing his Ph.D. in Rehabilitation Counselor Education at the University of Iowa. He remains involved in volunteer activities, which allow him to express his gratitude for the support others have given him.

SECTION IV

♦OVERCOMING EMOTIONAL♦ TRAUMA

The Scream by Edvard Munch, 1895

"Courage is sometimes frail as hope is frail: a fragile shoot between two stones that grows brave toward the sun though warmth and brightness fail, striving and faith the only strength it knows."
—FRANCES RODMAN

LIKE LEAPING OFF A MOUNTAIN
Karen Fisher

Nineteen years old, married six months to an Illinois dairy farmer, and five months pregnant, I was hiding in a feed room, as a cow was being stabbed with a pitchfork. The blood was running in rivulets down her legs, making puddles around her hooves. My husband was teaching her—and me—a lesson. He got a lead pipe and beat her nose, screaming, "YOU B—CH! YOU DON'T DO WHAT I TELL YOU!" The cow bellowed in fear and pain, the blood and drool flying, her hooves skidding in manure and blood, her body slamming against the cast-iron stanchion that held her. My husband finally exhausted himself and turned his screams to me: "GET OUT HERE NOW AND FEED THESE COWS!"

I waited until he had gone to release my tears so he wouldn't have the satisfaction of seeing me cry. The odor of the wounded cow's blood turned my stomach. Ever so gently, I put the feed in front of her and watched it change color from the blood dripping out of her nose.

I was no stranger to my husband's anger. Since our honeymoon, he had been screeching orders at me with a rage that baffled me. Soon the "accidents" had begun—the cupboard door flung open in my face, the gate that knocked me down as he shoved it over a fence. Despite my growing distress, I had been clinging to the hope that things would get better, knowing that no one in my family had ever divorced.

That day in the feed room, however, I witnessed my husband's violence toward animals for the first time. That day, I learned the meaning of terror, and a part of me froze. I could not speak of what I had seen, could not even bear to think of it. And although my husband never beat me or threatened directly to harm me, after that day I believed that this was a man capable of killing me if I provoked him or tried to leave. So I lowered my eyes, turned off my feelings, and went away somewhere inside myself where he couldn't get to me.

My days were filled with his screaming, bleeding animals and bone-breaking work. And with each day that passed, I lost more of my sense of self.

After my baby's birth, I found I could nurse him and sing to him in relative peace. My baby became my refuge and my reason to keep going. Soon the baby became a little boy. One evening, he toddled into the room where my husband sat. His little cup dribbled milk on the manure-covered jeans of his father, who responded by shrieking obscenities at him. Instantly, I was in front of my husband, my finger pointed in his face. A voice from some primal place inside me spoke in careful, measured tones, "Don't you ever speak to him that way again."

Something changed that day. My husband knew that he couldn't hurt my child, and I found a strength I didn't know I had. With that newfound strength I attempted my first escape. My parents, thinking we had merely quarreled, sent me back to him to try and work things out. Always controlling and critical, my husband became worse after my return. If someone complimented my cooking, he would comment, "She always burns the pan." He made me account for every penny I spent. He isolated me from my family and friends. "Who was here?" he demanded once after being away for a while. "I don't know. The meter reader, maybe," I replied. "No, that's not his tracks," he insisted. I realized then that he had memorized the tire treads of our routine visitors, so he could examine the mud in our driveway for signs of unauthorized guests.

During the next five years, I had two more beautiful children. My husband took so little interest in the kids that he didn't even know their middle names. But they were everything to me. I was determined that their lives were going to be happy, even if my own was miserable, and I poured my soul into being a good mother. I knew every trick in the book for making the children's socks sparkling white. We baked cookies together, watched *Sesame Street* together, read books together. I avoided my husband as much as possible, my resentment toward him increasing with each passing year.

Finally, I found the courage to attempt another escape. I went again to my parents. After a few days, my husband called, informing me that a lawyer had told him he could take the children away if I left him. It never occurred to me that he was lying. So against my mother's tearful pleas I went back. I was determined, however, that the next time I left, I'd succeed. I had to succeed, for I could not endure much more. Although the arrival of another baby delayed my departure, I prepared to make my move.

Money was a big reason I stayed as long as I did. My husband controlled all our assets. I had only a high school education and four children, two still in diapers. On top of that, I suffered from a learning disability known as dyslexia and thought of myself as dumb. How would I support myself and my children? Raised with a strong work ethic, I didn't consider government assistance an option. I will never forget one of my rare visits with my mom and two aunts. As we plotted my leaving, I proposed a solution I considered preposterous: "Well, what should I do then? Just leave him and go on welfare?" To my surprise, the three of them replied, in unison, with a swift and resounding "YES!" I was astounded but relieved. Leaving my husband suddenly seemed within my reach.

The final push I needed came from my children's trusted pediatrician. In 11 years of marriage, I had never been to a movie or inside a library. Dr. Thompson was my one small link to the real world. Soon after my baby was weaned, I found the courage to talk to him about how my husband treated me. He picked up the phone and began dialing a number. "That sounds like domestic violence," he said, "I'm calling the shelter"—and he held the receiver out to me. Until that moment, I had not known that shelters for abused women existed. I had not even known that I was abused! Abuse to me meant women with two black eyes and bruises all over their bodies, not the verbal bullying and tyranny I lived with.

Taking that phone from Dr. Thompson was like leaping off the largest mountain on earth. I didn't know if I would fly or die abruptly, but I knew I had to leap. I never actually lived at the shelter, but the folks there helped me start divorce proceedings. The divorce papers, carefully timed to arrive when the children and I were visiting my parents, were accompanied by a restraining order that forced my husband to move out.

Still his hovering in my life was oppressive. He made excuses to be at the farm constantly. Although he was not allowed in our yard, he would show up whenever I left the house and harangue me in the driveway. He made obsessive phone calls. His manic-depressive brother—who had tried to throw his own wife out a window—boasted that he would shoot me, and showed up on court dates to intimidate me. Stressed to my limit, I lost 40 pounds, and my hair started falling out in handfuls. But I was backed by an army of helpers: my extended family, my one close friend, Dr. Thompson, teachers and principals and a support group at the shelter. I held firm, gained custody of my kids, and eventually moved to a small town where every policeman on the force learned my ex-husband's license plate number and looked out for me.

I'd made it out. I was alive. But I was having nightmares in which I heard my ex-husband slamming a door, screaming my name, stealing my children. I would awaken in a cold sweat, my heart pounding so hard the blankets shook. Night after night, I comforted myself by thinking of my childhood room, the purple room in the house my daddy had built from the ground up. I imagined the smell of summer in my room, the swell of the curtain in the breeze, the sound of crickets, and the slow, rhythmic "whoo whoo whoo" of an owl. Finally I taught myself to sleep again, taught myself that I was stronger than the bad dreams.

I started drawing the things I had never been able to say out loud. I drew the blood in the cow feed, I drew the terror, beginning the journey back from the faraway place where I had hidden myself. Then I learned to type. Because of my dyslexia, writing with pen or pencil had always been a chore. But as I typed, 11 years of pain and fear poured out of me. Late at night, after the children were in bed, I typed. As I found my voice, I shook, and often I cried, tears soaking the front of my pajamas. And before long, I was able to begin talking about the animals, the final step in freeing myself from the demons that haunted me while I slept.

Meanwhile I had decided that in order to support my children, I must get a college degree. The folks at the welfare office told me that I would lose my government support if I went back to school. With pit-bull tenacity, I kept after them until they decided to make an exception in my case. So while living on $607 per month and raising four children, I began college fulltime. My wonderful parents helped with childcare. Balancing my responsibilities was sometimes tough, but it was a cakewalk compared to my previous life. The hardest part of college was convincing myself that I could do it.

I remember my first-semester literature class. The professor handed back our initial assignment, a two-page commentary on a book we were reading. I sat in dread of the low grade I was sure I'd gotten. I thought to myself: *What on earth am I doing here? I'm too stupid to go to college.*

The professor's voice broke through my self-disparagement: "Karen, would you read your paper out loud for us?" Convinced she was going to critique my work in front of the whole class, I somehow got to my feet and began reading: "*The Invisible Man* reminds me of the women I have met in domestic violence support groups."

As I finished—after what seemed like a million years—I was shocked to hear my professor say, "I had Karen read her paper as an example of excellent work."

After class, I walked to my car in a bewildered trance. There must be some mistake; I didn't know how to write. About halfway home, however, a Cheshire-cat smile crept onto my face. It wasn't just good work, it was excellent work! Maybe I could do this college thing, after all.

I graduated three and a half years later, *magna cum laude*, with a bachelor's degree in Social Work. I was employed immediately, and joyfully went off AFDC. For the last two years I have run a program to aid the homeless and others in crisis. My children are healthy and happy, and I have terrific friends.

I used to say I wouldn't wish my life on my worst enemy. But now, though my life has been harder than some, I wouldn't trade my experience for the world. The bad part provided a contrast for the richness I now have. Sometimes, like all of us, I have moments of discouragement, when I feel like a very small goldfish swimming up Niagara Falls. When that happens, I picture those falls pounding, and I picture myself as a tiny spot of coppery orange, beating my way furiously toward the top. Just one little goldfish, with bright, shining words tucked away inside: "Excellent work."

Karen Fisher lives in Evansville, Wisconsin with her four children. While working part-time, she recently obtained a Masters degree.

RECLAIMING MY SOUL
Linda Langstraat

One September Sunday, my friends and family gathered for a "soul-warming," a celebration of my transcendence of the most traumatic experience of my life. In a beautiful ritual, guests took turns pouring salt water, symbolizing tears of grief transformed to joy, into a crystal bowl. They also spoke to me about my strength and growth. My friend Houston told me that if he were a Gospel writer, he would write the Book of Linda, the story of my courage in dealing with trauma.

The trauma my friend referred to had occurred more than a decade before, when I was 40 years old. It is not an easy story to hear but I believe that with each telling I heal emotionally a little more, and so I continue to tell it.

I was single and living alone. Late one October night, I stepped onto my back porch to call my cat. A man leaped out of hiding and hooked his arm around my throat, hissing that he would kill me if I made a sound. He dragged me inside and doused the lights in every room. He threw me on my bed and tore off my clothes. "Call me Daddy," he insisted, as he raped me and I choked back sobs of terror.

Afterward, he tore my house apart looking for valuables. He threatened to slash me with my own 10-inch butcher knife. Then he raped me again. At the end of a nightmare hour, he tied a pillow around my face so that I couldn't scream or see and could barely breathe. He tore a sheet into strips and bound my wrists so tightly that I soon had no feeling in my hands. As I lay on my stomach on my bed, he tied my hands together with my feet. Finally, he took a chair and brutally beat my legs and arms.

After my assailant left, driving away in my new car, I slid down to the floor. I was naked, in pain, and terribly cold, because the rapist had set my air conditioner at full blast. I felt huge relief that he was gone but was also afraid that he might come back. My worst fear, however, was that I might not be able to get loose. It was the beginning of the weekend. It might be days before someone got worried and came looking for me. Would I lose my hands from lack of circulation? Could I die?

I thought of getting a knife in order to cut my bonds. The pillow, though still tied round my head, had shifted enough that I could see. I moved laboriously toward the kitchen on my knees. I was exhausted by the time I reached the threshold between dining room and kitchen. How could I cross the hard linoleum kitchen floor? And how could I open a drawer to retrieve a knife? The obstacles seemed insurmountable, and I fell to the dining room carpet. I lay there for the next three hours, my head resting on the pillow that had nearly suffocated me.

At last I remembered the scissors I had left on my ironing board in the spare bedroom. Lying on my side, I inched my body toward that room until I reached the ironing board. Perhaps I could tilt it enough to make the scissors drop to the floor. The trick would be to avoid causing the iron to fall on me. I weakly pushed the board, and succeeded in tipping the scissors off. Miraculously, the iron stayed in place.

I am right-handed, but my right hand was completely numb and useless. However, I had slight movement in my left hand. Despite the pain—I discovered later my elbow was broken—I was able to grasp the scissors with my left hand. I opened the shears a tiny bit and snipped at the sheeting that bound me. Painstakingly, I cut the binding, one thread at a time, until I severed it and freed my legs. Then—I don't remember how—I somehow cut my hands apart.

As quickly as I was able, I dressed and ran to my neighbors' house, rousing them from bed. They built a fire to warm me and

ESCAPE FROM SLAVERY

Henry "Box" Brown was born a slave in 1815 on a plantation near Richmond, Virginia. He was separated from his parents and siblings at the age of 15, when they were sold to different owners. At the age of 24, he was again devastated by the loss of loved ones when his wife and children were sold and taken to North Carolina. Determined to free himself from the heartless tyranny of his lot, he ran away and found a sympathetic storekeeper to help him make his way to Philadelphia, where the storekeeper had contact with an abolitionist group. Brown came up with the idea of having himself shipped to Philadelphia in a wooden box, three by two and a half feet in size. The following is Brown's account of his journey, which took 27 hours and earned him the admiring sobriquet, "Box."

'Arrangements were made for my departure, and I took my place in this narrow prison, with a mind full of uncertainty as to the result. It was a critical period of my life, I can assure you, reader; but if you have never been deprived of your liberty, as I was, you cannot realize the power of that hope of freedom, which was to me indeed, 'an anchor to the soul, both sure and steadfast' . . .

"With no access to the fresh air, excepting three small gimlet holes, I started on my perilous cruise. I was first carried to the express office, the box being placed on its end, so that I started with my head downward, although the box was directed: 'This side up with care.' "

After being transferred to the baggage car of a train, where he traveled right side up, Brown was again placed on his head, aboard a steamboat: "In this dreadful position, I remained the space of an hour and a half, it seemed to me, when I began to feel of my eyes and head, and found to my dismay, that my eyes were almost swollen out of their sockets, and the veins on my temple seemed ready to burst. I endured the terrible pain, as well as I could, sustained under the whole by the thoughts of sweet liberty. About half an hour afterwards, I attempted again to lift my hands to my face, but I found I was not able to move them. A cold sweat now covered me from head to foot. Death seemed my inevitable fate but I lifted up my heart to God in prayer, believing that he would yet deliver me, when to my joy, I overheard two men say, 'We have been here two hours and have traveled 20 miles, now let us sit down, and rest ourselves.' They suited the action to the word, and turned the box over, containing my soul and body, thus delivering me from the power of the grim messenger of death . . .

"Soon after this fortunate event, we arrived at Washington, where I was thrown from a wagon, and again as my luck would have it, fell on my head. I was then rolled down a declivity, until I reached the platform from which the cars were to start. During this short but rapid journey, my neck came very near being dislocated. I was then tumbled into the car, my head downwards again, as I seemed to be destined to escape on my head. We had not proceeded far, however, before more baggage was placed in the car and I was again turned to my proper position."

After arriving in Philadelphia, Brown was delivered to his destination, where a number of sympathizers took tools and removed the cover of his box: "The first impulse of my soul, as I looked around, and beheld my friends was to break out in a song of deliverance, and praise to the most high God. My labor was accomplished, my warfare was ended, and I stood erect before my equal fellow men, no longer a crouching slave."

Brown's words are excerpted from an account published in the Afro-Amercian Encyclopedia *(Educational Book Publishers, 1974).*

called the police, who arrived immediately to take my story, gather evidence and get me medical attention.

The events of that night in October took place over five hours. Recovering from the emotional trauma of that night took 11 years.

Initially, I moved in a fog, unable to concentrate or think clearly. I couldn't accomplish routine tasks like cooking or paying my bills. I barely functioned at my job. As each night approached, I felt anxious, frightened to leave my house for any reason. I lost weight and had trouble sleeping. And sadly, I lost the fun part of myself, the part that laughed and felt alive and enjoyed being with friends.

My rapist remained at large. I hadn't seen his face clearly in

> *"He has not learned the lesson of life who does not every day surmount a fear."*
> —Ralph Waldo Emerson

the darkness of my house, but I had memorized the shape of his ear. Although I identified a suspect for the police, he was soon released, because his hair did not match the DNA of a hair found in my bed. The knowledge that the rapist was roaming free increased my sense of terror.

For many months after the rape, members of my church fed me, kept me company, and slept over at my house, until I could begin taking care of myself again. After struggling at my job for nearly a year, I took a six-month leave of absence. I refused to leave the neighborhood I loved—I refused to give the rapist the power to make me leave!—but I did move eventually to a house several blocks away where I felt safer. Gradually, during the first two years following the rape, I resumed functioning. But I was hardly back to normal.

Despite friends who were impatient for me to act like my old self, I was determined not to pretend I was fine when I was depressed or appear strong when I felt weak. In fact, I prayed to be brave enough to allow myself to be weak. It was by acknowledging my black times and neediness that I was able to find my way through them.

I attended support groups at a rape crisis center. Later, I entered therapy. Over and over, I pushed myself to talk about my rape, my fear and my despair for the sake of my emotional recovery. A necessary part of getting better was learning to express an emotion I'd always been afraid of: anger. My therapist suggested pounding a pillow as a stand-in for my rapist. I would beat that pillow for all I was worth, shouting at my rapist, "NO, NO, NO, NO, NO! YOU CAN'T DO THIS TO ME!"

I was also angry at God. "God can take your anger, Linda," my pastor encouraged me.

And so I confronted Him, too: "How could you let his happen to me?" I raged. "When am I ever going to feel right again?"

Letting my anger out, I was able to let it go.

The culmination of my efforts occurred about ten years after the rape. My sister, Janice, had been urging me to participate in a two-week self-defense course in Helena, Montana, where she lives. Janice would be assisting the instructor during the course. I was not keen on the idea at first. Although I am 5 feet seven, I am small-boned and not very muscular. But I finally found the courage to try it.

During the course, I learned to stomp on an assailant's instep, throw him off balance, knee him in the groin and get him down, then knock him out with a knee blow to his head. Our instructor would dress up in huge amounts of padding, so that you couldn't actually hurt him, but he could tell by the force of your knee blows whether you'd delivered a knockout punch. My graduation exercise was a reenactment of the assault. As I pretended to call my cat, I was petrified. The instructor grabbed me from behind and spit out the rapist's first words, "Shut up b—ch, or I'll kill you." Despite my terror, I tackled him, using all my new skill—and knocked him out in 20 seconds flat.

Shortly after I completed the course, I had a dream. I was cooking a huge, ugly, very old fish in my microwave. I cooked it forever. Then, all of a sudden, the window of the microwave shattered and the fish came flying through the window and landed on the floor. At first it was still; then it started to twitch. And out of the fish popped a kitten, a soft, playful, frisky kitten.

I feel that dream was about me, that the fish was the horror of my life after the rape and that the kitten was the emergence of new life and joy.

Today my life is good. I'm not afraid to stay out late. I laugh with friends. And I continue to reclaim my power. Just this week, I realized that for all these years I've avoided shopping for a kitchen knife to replace the one my rapist stole. I think that now I'm ready to buy a new knife.

Linda Langstraat has lived in Atlanta for the past 21 years. She developed and is director of the Adopt-a-Grandparent Program, a service that matches inner-city senior citizens with adult volunteers who minister to their needs for companionship.

> "Although the world is full of suffering,
> it is full also of the overcoming of it."
> —Helen Keller

ILMA'S STORY
Marilyn Greenberg

Author's Note: *I work in a community college in northern California, teaching students with head injuries or learning disabilities. Ilma Watson was my student. In addition to having a brain injury, she was poorly educated in her first language, Portuguese, and had little formal education in English. Yet she persevered in her studies in a way that won my wholehearted admiration. This is Ilma's story, in her voice, based on notes from interviews with her.*

I grew up in a poor neighborhood in Rio de Janeiro, on a street crowded with rickety houses. I remember weekend evenings, standing on tiptoe at a window in one of our three tiny rooms, my heels raised above the hard dirt floor, my eyes barely clearing the window ledge, trying to catch a glimpse of the festivities out back. My handsome, intelligent Daddy, always eager to make money, had set up lantern-lit tables on our patio, turning it into a nightclub. Loud music and Daddy's laughter filled the air. My sister and I wanted to join him and my five brothers in serving drinks, but we girls were not allowed near the rowdy dancing.

I wished I could remember Mommy. She had died giving birth to my younger brother when I was two, and there was only an empty space when I thought of her. But not when I thought of Daddy. His smile lit my days and nights, even when he was gone, working at the market or as a security guard.

When I was 12, my world turned upside down. Daddy got sick and had to go to the hospital. One Sunday, my sister returned in tears from visiting him. "Daddy is dead! Daddy is dead!" she sobbed. I raced past her through the streets to his hospital room. It was empty. I crawled under the bed, wailing, "I want my Daddy back!"

In the days following Daddy's death, I yearned to follow him. Every night, I lay on his bed, calling him. One night the bed shook. Chills coursed through my body, and I saw my father. His spirit told me that I could not follow him yet, but he promised he would come back for me when I was old. His words filled me with despair for I did not want to wait.

I went to live with one of my older brothers but before the year was over, he beat me and threw me out. I moved in with my Daddy's old girlfriend but left after a few days, when her new husband tried to force himself on me. Finally, I went to my godmother. She insisted that I work, so I found a job as a live-in maid for a wealthy family. From sunup until nine at night I did housework and minded the children. Sunday, my one free day, I went home to my godmother—until our falling out.

I often hung out at a nightclub after work. One evening, I returned to my employer's home too late and found the doors locked. I went to my godmother's house but was afraid to wake her, so I slept on the step outside her doorway.

"What are you doing here?" my godmother demanded when she answered my knock at her door the next morning. I had barely begun to explain when she called me a liar and accused me of sleeping with men. "Whore!" she screamed at me, as she tore my clothes from my body. Then she grabbed a leather belt and began whipping me. "Whore!" she continued shrieking, so loudly that the whole neighborhood could hear, and she opened the door and pushed me outside, naked for all to see.

I left her that day and never went back. I left my job, too. That's when I started living in the street. My home was a sidewalk, a park bench, any place I could sleep for free. I sneaked inside apartment buildings and slept on concrete stairways.

Sometimes I wandered the streets of Rio de Janeiro until night-time. I became friends with other girls like myself, tough slum girls who spent their lives in the streets, on the beach, and hanging around the lake, looking for trouble just for the fun of it, starting fights for no reason.

I didn't care about myself. I only wanted to die. So I started drinking heavily, hoping that would kill me. Sometimes it eased my pain. But I didn't die. Desperate, I jumped off a 30-foot cliff near the lake. Landing in the thick brush below, I barely got hurt.

Thoughts of death continued to fill my mind, and I continued to place myself in risky situations. If I couldn't die by my own hands, perhaps others would do the job for me. But the police only jailed me when they caught me, a reckless 16-year-old, stealing bread and milk from the doorstep of an expensive home. In prison, I was often beaten by the guards but they, too, stopped short of killing me.

By the time I was 22, little had changed in my life. After being released from prison, I worked at a string of housekeeping jobs and hung out after work with my old crowd. Depressed and embittered, I was still drinking heavily. At Christmas that year, I got drunk on champagne, poured gasoline on myself and lit a match. My clothes caught fire but miraculously my body was unharmed. Only my waist was singed from the band of my blackened skirt.

Why was I unable to end my miserable life? Every time I had tried to kill myself, I had been saved. I realized then that my father's spirit must be protecting me and that I was meant to live to a ripe old age. I had been given the strength to survive many ordeals. Perhaps I could use that strength to make my life more bearable.

First, I decided to stop drinking, for alcohol led me into self-destructive actions and no longer eased my pain. Next I looked for a better job. This time I wouldn't settle for the first thing that came along. I had to find something better than the conditions offered by my employers, who were so unfair that they were charging me, a live-in maid, for my living expenses.

I began working for a wonderful family who treated me like one of their own. When I got sick they called the doctor and made sure I got the proper blood tests. They gave me money to shop for lunch or dinner and never asked how much I spent. For the first time since Daddy's death, I started caring about myself. When my gang friends came to visit, I told them to stay away. I was growing stronger and protecting myself, despite the times when yearning thoughts of death crept into my mind to plague me.

When I was 26, I had a chance to come to the United States. I had taken care of Juana, a friend, while she was recovering from injuries received in a traffic accident. In return, she offered to ask her sister, who lived in the United States, to help me find a job in this country. The thought of leaving the only family I had known since I was 12 brought tears to my eyes. But the dream of bettering my life was stronger than my sadness and fears, so I accepted Juana's offer.

I had become an expert cook over the years. I always watched what people did and copied it and changed it to the way I liked it. I don't know how to measure or weigh food. I just put everything together to make a meal. As a result of this talent, it wasn't long before I had a job as a cook with the Consulate of the Brazilian Embassy in Washington, D.C. It may sound glamorous but it was hard work, doing all the cooking, serving, and cleaning for up to 30 people! And I didn't get paid much. It was a beginning, but after three years, I quit that job, determined to improve my lot, and started catering and cleaning houses and office buildings. I still worked hard and long, with never a holiday, but I was making decent money for the first time in my life—and I was my own boss!

I married briefly, at 31, and had a son. After my delivery,

when the nurse brought me my newborn baby, I almost fainted. He had Daddy's face. I knew that Daddy had come back in Jerry. I no longer had to follow Daddy for he was here with me. Finally, the self-hating anger that had smoldered in me for years was gone, and I was able to leave behind my lingering thoughts of death. Although my life might not be easy, I would be there for my son—and for myself.

Ilma met one of the greatest tests of her strength 10 years later. By this time, she had moved to California. Biking along a country road in Sonoma County one day, she hit a patch of gravel, lost her balance, and fell to the ground, severely injuring her head. As a result, Ilma has permanent damage to one side of her brain. Subsequently, she enrolled in a community college program that helped her regain her skills as a professional cook. Throughout this ordeal, she continued, with the help of friends, to parent Jerry.

Today, Ilma is 54. Her son recently graduated from college, and Ilma works in the college cafeteria. In 1999 she became an American citizen. Sitting in her cozy, peaceful apartment—so different from her closet-sized maid's rooms in Rio de Janeiro—Ilma reflects on her past and future:

When I was younger I felt I had no future. Today I believe in my future more than ever. I want to graduate from high school and then from community college. I know that with my head injury I will have to work much harder than the other students in my classes. But I have a goal: I want to work with teenagers in gangs who hate themselves and their lives. I've been there, and I have a lot to offer. My father has been my guardian angel. Perhaps he saved me so that I can be a guardian angel to others.

Marilyn Greenberg is a learning facilitator at Santa Rosa Junior College. She lives with her husband and daughter in northern California.

A PRAYER

Refuse to fall down.

If you cannot refuse to fall down,

refuse to stay down.

If you cannot refuse to stay down,

lift your heart toward heaven,

and like a hungry beggar,

ask that it be filled,

and it will be filled.

You may be pushed down.

You may be kept from rising.

But no one can keep you

from lifting your heart

toward heaven—

only you.

It is in the midst of misery

that so much becomes clear.

The one who says nothing good

came of this,

is not yet listening.

—Clarissa Pinkola Estés

Clarissa Pinkola Estés is the author of *Women Who Run with the Wolves* and *The Faithful Gardener*, from which this poem was taken.

INVISIBLE NO MORE
Pam Conkling

T he most difficult thing I did as a child was going home. In grade school, when the day was over I stayed on the playground as long as possible, swinging or jumping rope, mentally willing the other children not to leave. For when they were gone, it would be time for me to leave, too. When I could stall no longer, I trudged slowly homeward, my dread mounting with each block. Reaching our house, I forced my legs to the front door, then lingered, staring at the doorknob before grasping it and entering. Neither of my parents was there yet: My mother worked evenings; my father would come in at 4:30.

Retreating to my room at the end of the hall, I climbed to the top of my bunk bed, where I sat rocking, legs crossed Indian-style, listening for my father's return. When I heard his key in the lock, my body became rigidly alert. How angry would he be today? How bad would it be for me and my brother and sister? Often, he came in raging: "G-D—T, WHO LEFT THIS SWEATER ON THE COUCH?" In terror, holding my breath, I tried to prepare myself for a beating as my father marched down the hall toward my room, cussing and loudly counting off the number of times he intended to strike me.

One of my father's favorite ways of punishing us was hitting us with his fraternity paddle, which he kept hanging in his bedroom next to his dresser. Almost two feet long and eight inches wide, this paddle was so thick it never broke, even when my father hit us 50 times in a row. "Assume the position," my father would order, indicating that we were to spread our legs and bend over; and then he would hit us. And once he started, he didn't seem able to stop.

It did not take much to provoke Dad's ire. When I was a second-grader, he announced that I was going to learn to tell time. I sat down, eager at the prospect of learning such a grownup skill, and my father handed me a watch, with no explanation of how to interpret the numbers and hands on its face. "What time is it?" he demanded.

"I don't know," I responded. At this answer, my father hit me. "What time is it?" he demanded again.

"I don't know," I replied, weeping. And he hit me again. And again, and again.

Things were no better when my mother was home. At best, she stayed put in her bedroom, lost in an alcoholic stupor. If alert, she was our jailer, locking the door to prevent us escaping as my dad fetched his paddle. Then there were the times when she became a vengeful harpie, spewing harsh words, washing our mouths out with soap, or striking out at us. These times tended to occur during her sporadic attempts to stop drinking, and I learned to watch her hands for trembling, the certain sign that her craving had become intolerable.

Our home was like a concentration camp, and we kids didn't dare talk—even to each other—about our family's awful secrets. For deep in our hearts, we truly believed that if we made him mad enough, our father was capable of killing us.

I entered adulthood in a state of shock. Having received so little nurturing, I had never learned to pay attention to my own needs or what went on inside me. If the palsied hands of an elderly neighbor triggered a flashback to a scene with my drink-deprived mother, I dismissed it from awareness, conscious only of a vague panic and sweat-soaked underarms. If disturbing dreams woke me several nights a week, I told myself that everyone had nightmares. If I was unhappy, I ignored my feelings or withdrew to my bedroom. In most situations, I tried to stay invisible, keeping my voice very small and telling myself I had nothing to say.

Feelings of anger—my own or others'—presented special difficulties. On the rare occasions when I recognized a resentment in myself, I did not dare stand up on my own behalf, for I might incur someone's disapproval. And if others were displeased, I suddenly felt like a terrified child, helplessly facing my father's fury. To avoid such feelings, I turned myself inside out, trying to keep others happy. If my husband was grouchy because he'd lost sleep getting up with our baby in the middle of the night, I quickly took full responsibility for that duty. If he came home out of sorts from a bad day at the office, I felt an urgent need to fix his problems and spent the evening anxiously bombarding him with advice.

At my job, I could not tolerate any situation that might involve a confrontation. One time, when I was working as a copyeditor, my boss put me in charge of tracking the mistakes of my coworkers. For days I wrestled with my dilemma, my stomach tied in knots. If I carried out my assignment, I might get my coworkers in trouble; if I talked with my boss about my reluctance to do the task he'd given me, I might make him mad. Unwilling to risk either outcome, I resigned.

The arrival of my two sons stirred up painful memories. As I swept spilled Cheerios from the area surrounding their highchairs, for instance, I became filled with apprehension, reliving dinners in my own childhood. My father would routinely single out the child he judged to be the messiest eater. That child was then forced to crawl about on hands and knees, cleaning fallen crumbs from the floor with his or her mouth, as my father made humiliating jokes about human vacuum cleaners.

I was determined to give my boys the love I had never had. But one day, my brother-in-law, a doctor, said to me, "Pam, you seem depressed." I hadn't realized until then how unhappy I was, but I knew at once he was right. How could I make my boys happy if I was miserable myself?

> *"Courage takes many forms. There is physical courage; there is moral courage. Then there is still a higher type of courage— the courage to brave pain, to live with it, to never let others know of it and to still find joy in life."*
> —Howard Cosell

My brother-in-law's comment was a gift I hadn't known I needed, and I decided to seek help. Haltingly, I began to share my family's ugly secrets with a therapist and to look at the legacy of my parents' abuse. "There's a hurt, scared little girl inside you who wants your understanding and support," my therapist told me. "Part of your job is to listen and figure out what she needs, so she can finally feel parented. And as you do that, you'll find you're able to parent your boys better, too."

Gradually I started becoming more assertive, convinced now that my sons and my own inner child needed a parent strong enough to speak up. "I don't appreciate you saying that," I forced myself to tell my husband when he made a sarcastic remark about my math skills. "I need my sleep, and I can't talk now," I told my mother, when she phoned me, drunk, in the middle of the night. And although my heart fluttered in my chest, I mustered all my courage and spoke to a friend who disapproved of my being in therapy. "I know you believe that prayer and faith in God should be enough. But my therapy is a God-given lifeline for me, and I can't be friends with you unless you can support my choice."

One great challenge to my budding strength occurred during a family vacation. We were staying at a campground, and I had just finished cleaning up after breakfast. As I hung the dishtowels out to dry, I noticed a boy, maybe 14 years old, who was staying in the campsite next to ours. He was packing up the salt,

WE FORGET

We forget that stars are born in wild blasts
that seeds blown far are more likely to last
that beginnings are chaotic.

And so we go for the comfort of order
each day stay with our ritual way
get up first
let out the dogs
lift weights, choose between the treadmill and the bike
exchange the same small kisses
don't eat the things we like
to hold off chaos as if it were an enemy about to strike.

Then stumbling at an impasse
when someone dies or we fall from grace
afraid, ugly and alone
searching
for a way back home
we discover that order was the brick boundary
at the end of a road
obscuring the view,
and chaos our clay to form and lay
a graceful new path
to peace.

—Maggie Anderson

Maggie Anderson is a corporate communications consultant.

pepper and other condiments on his site's picnic table. Suddenly his father charged out the trailer door and came up behind him. *Crack!* He struck his son on the neck so hard that it sounded as if a tree had been hit by lightning, and the boy fell to the ground. I froze, my legs weak, as the man returned to the trailer. The surrounding campsites had grown eerily quiet.

I have to do something, I said to myself, although my first impulse was to jump into my car and flee as far as possible from the violence I had just witnessed. Despite my terror that at any moment he would reemerge and catch me in the act, I wrote down his license number and descriptions of his car and trailer. As the man and his family got into their car and pulled out of the campground, I went to the park office and called the police. *What if they slip up and he finds out who reported him?* I thought, as I responded, in a shaky voice, to the police officer's questions about my name, address, and phone number. But as the policeman told me that someone would track the family down on the highway and check on the boy's safety, I felt a surge of relief. *Yes!* I silently exclaimed.

No one ever "gets over" a childhood like mine. I still have nightmares and flashbacks and anxiety attacks, although less frequently than before. But I proved that day that I could overcome my fear in order to protect an abused child. I proved to the little girl within that I was strong enough to protect her. And I showed myself that I could change and grow and find my voice.

Pam Conkling lives in Acworth, Georgia, and she is studying to obtain a counseling degree.

SECTION V

♦ THE WAY WE WERE AT WAR ♦

*"Bravery is the capacity to perform
properly even when scared half to death."*
—OMAR BRADLEY

LIKE A SHADOW
Wayne R. "Crash" Coe

Among my memories of Vietnam, the night of the 14th of January 1968 stands out. More than 30 years later, the thought of it brings beads of sweat to my brow.

I was a young Warrant Officer Pilot flying for the 120th Assault Helicopter Company, known as the Deans. Despite the unit's venerable history in developing helicopter warfare, by the time I joined the Saigon-based unit, it was primarily a taxi service, hauling VIPs from Washington to look in on our troops in the field. I had seen plenty of combat during my time in Nam, and this assignment was a wonderful change. I had a room instead of a tent, hot water some of the time and access to the oriental delicacies sold in the Cholon area shops and eateries.

As an added bonus, I lived close to my best friend in Vietnam, Major David Royal Warden, our 13th Group Flight Surgeon, who had previously been in the same unit as I. Although he was a doctor, Warden—we called him "Doc"—had flown with me many times; my former platoon leader had put him on the rotation to give some of the other pilots a break. Like me, he had a new assignment—in Long Binh, just down the road from Saigon.

As luck would have it that January night, Doc was at the controls of my helicopter as we awaited permission to take off from the main airbase in Saigon. My mission was to pick up a passenger at Bien Hoa and drop him off at U.S. Army headquarters in Long Binh. Then I would drop Doc Warden off at his quarters and bring the helicopter back to the airbase.

Helicopter night flights in Vietnam were not for the squeamish. Helicopters are inherently unstable, and when you add poor visibility and unseen obstacles, the combination can be fatal. But I had complete confidence in Doc.

"Dean Four Three, ready for takeoff," I announced over the mike, identifying myself to the control tower.

The answer came back: "Dean 43, you are number two for takeoff behind the Razor Back fire team helicopters on the ready pad." I looked over to see the ammunition-heavy C model gunships "pulling pitch"—increasing power to their rotor blades while they skidded down the runway, gathering speed for takeoff. I thought to myself: Someone must be stepping in shit tonight; the Razor Backs don't fly at night for their amusement. I followed their helicopters out, then turned east while the guns stayed low and headed north.

It was a beautiful and cool evening. Unlike the gunships, we were carrying only two small machine guns, and the helicopter climbed to 1500 feet in a matter of seconds. I was trying to get the armed forces radio tuned in for the crew to listen to, when Doc's West Virginia drawl came over the intercom, drawing our attention to the highway below. "Looks like a truck convoy stalled down there," he said, "with a huge volume of tracers and concussion rings coming off it."

It was obvious the convoy of trucks was being ambushed. The adrenaline hit my brain like a grenade going off. I carried a list of radio frequencies that covered everyone with a radio in South Vietnam. I looked up the convoy frequency and quickly punched it up on the FM radio.

"Red Rider, Red Rider. Dean 43 is over your location. Do you need some help?"

"Dean 43, Red Rider 6. We are being ambushed and are pinned down. We could use a medivac and some gun support."

I went to the emergency frequency: "Razor Back fire team, Dean 43, we have convoy under attack. Can you give me fire support?"

"Negative 43, we are too far away and we are expended, over."

"Paris Radar, Dean 43, over," I said, directing myself to the controllers who constantly tracked us on their radarscope.

"Go ahead, Dean 43: We have been monitoring your radio calls."

"Can you get me a gun team? I am squawking 777, 20 miles east of Saigon, over."

"Roger, 43: We have positive contact and are scrambling a Playboy fire team from Bien Hoa. Over."

"Dean 43, Red Rider."

"Go ahead, Red Rider."

"The driver of our lead truck is hit in the head but still breathing and we cannot get close enough to give aid—can you give me some fire suppression? Over."

"Roger, Red Rider, I am inbound." And with that we dove our UH-1H model right at the ambush! Doc was shooting out the door, my crew was working out with their M-60 machine guns, we were kicking the crap out of the ambush, and the Viet Cong stopped shooting for a minute and took cover. However, we knew it would not take the Viet Cong long to figure out we were not a gunship and continue to press their attack.

Doc Warden keyed the intercom: "If we don't get that wounded man out of there and into a hospital, he will be dead in a few minutes. If you can get me close, I'll go get him."

"I can get you close," I replied.

There were two sets of high-power lines running down the north side of the highway. We would have to go over one set of wires, but under the other set, to keep from exposing ourselves to enemy fire. We were not able to fire our M-60's because we might hit the men in the trucks, who were all on the north side of the road, shooting back at the Viet Cong.

It would have been suicide to turn on the landing light, so I had the crew hanging out the door, looking for wires and the ground coming up. My crew guided me in and while we were on short final approach, just before coming to a hover, Doc Warden unbuckled his harness and stepped out on the helicopter's skid. I could not find a place to land the helicopter so I stayed at a very low hover, and Doc jumped down and ran over to the truck with the wounded man in it.

When the Viet Cong realized that there was a helicopter on short final, just behind the trucks, they threw everything they had at us. I was close enough to the lead truck to see bullets hitting it all over and bullets ricocheting off the road under the truck. Fortunately, most of the fire was going over us, and our helicopter was unscratched so far.

David Warden is the coolest man I have ever seen under fire. An All-American college football star before going to med school, he was as big and strong as a draft horse. He gently pulled the wounded driver out of the driver's seat, holding him in his massive arms like a baby. The volume of fire being poured at him was horrific, and I was sure I was going to see my best friend die before my eyes. He then ran down the embankment straight at the helicopter. I turned the helicopter so the door was facing him, and when he got real close, he jumped in the helicopter, still cradling the driver in his arms. All 250 pounds of him hit the floor with a thud. I did a pedal turn and went out the way I had come in, watching green tracers streaking down both sides of the helicopter, listening for the pop in the earphones that signifies a bullet strike to the aircraft.

Doc cradled the wounded driver in his arms so he could breathe and to restrain him from moving and injuring himself further. I called the 24th Evac hospital and told them the nature of the wounds, and they sent a team out to the pad to wait for us.

My crew chief had trained as a medic, and he and Doc Warden

ALAMO ALARM

T he Texas Revolution pitted Mexican forces against settlers who were trying to secure Texan independence from Mexico. The Alamo, a fort and former mission in San Antonio, had been captured by Texans in late 1835, but Mexican general Santa Ana was determined to retake it. For 13 days, Mexican troops, who greatly outnumbered the Texans, surrounded and attacked the fort. Finally, on March 6, 1836, Santa Ana's troops overran the fort, killing all 189 of its defenders, including legendary frontiersman Davy Crockett and knife fighter James Bowie. This call to arms was written at the beginning of the siege and dispatched by courier to nearby towns:

Commandancy of the Alamo, Texas
February 24, 1836

To the People of Texas and All Americans in the World

Fellow citizens and compatriots:
I am besieged by a thousand or more of the Mexicans under Santa Ana. I have sustained continual bombardment and cannonade for 24 hours and have not lost a man. The enemy has demanded a surrender at discretion; otherwise the garrison are to be put to the sword if the fort is taken. I have answered the demand with a cannon shot, and our flag still waves proudly from the walls. I shall never surrender nor retreat. Then, I call on you in the name of Liberty, of patriotism, and of everything dear to the American character, to come to our aid with all dispatch. The enemy is receiving reinforcements daily and will no doubt increase to three or four thousand in four or five days. If this call is neglected, I am determined to sustain myself as long as possible and die like a soldier who never forgets what is due to his own honor and that of his country.

Victory or Death
—William Barrett Travis
Lt. Col. Comdt

kept the wounded man alive until we touched down at the 24th Evac.

The men on the hospital pad stood by and watched as Doc Warden carried the wounded man, whose name was David Berry, into triage. I moved the helicopter off the active pad and shut down to look for battle damage. Miraculously, we were unscathed. However there was a huge pool of darkening blood on the floor of the aircraft.

When I went into triage to look for Doc Warden, they had already taken David Berry to surgery, and Doc was cleaning up a huge gash in his own leg. "When did that happen?" I asked.

He looked up over his glasses and said, "I don't remember; I didn't feel a thing. I thought all the blood was coming from David Berry."

So with one leg cut off Doc's fatigues, fresh bandages, and the blood cleaned off the floor, we went to Bien Hoa to look for our official passenger. Later, I took Doc back to the hospital so he could check in on Berry, who we knew might not make it through the night. He had found out that Berry was a Mormon, just like the two of us.

Doc called CW3 William Koerner, our Mormon group leader, and the two of them gave the unconscious Berry a blessing. Koerner prayed for Berry's survival and, for some reason—perhaps because of the nature of Berry's wound—he assumed that Berry's eyesight might be at risk. "Our Father in Heaven, please restore this soldier's vision and make him whole again," Koerner asked. What Bill Koerner did not know was that the neurosurgeons had just suctioned out the part of David Berry's brain that is called the optical lobe. I thought it was a pretty big order, even for God.

When Berry came out of the anesthetic, he was blind. I sat and talked with him about his family in Los Angeles, and the grocery store his father owned. He was especially concerned that, with his loss of sight, he would not be able to help at home with the family business.

Two days later I stopped in to see how Berry was doing. When I walked up to his bed he sat up and said, "You're taller than I expected."

"You can see me?" I asked, amazed.

"Not real clearly—more like a shadow," he replied.

But David Berry's vision improved every day. Today, he sees well enough to drive, although his vision is black and white only.

Too bad Bill Koerner was not more specific in his order.

Crash Coe lives on Florida's Gulf Coast. Putting his memories of Vietnam down on paper helps keep them from haunting him at night. He has been published on Internet sites, such as www.war-stories.com.

> *"Courage is fear that has said its prayers."*
> —Dorothy Bernard

DIVINE TACTICS

Many believe that the greatest war story ever told is the biblical tale of Gideon's victory found in the Old Testament *Book of Judges.*

An angel appeared to Gideon, an Israelite farmer, and announced that God wanted him to liberate his people from the Midianites, marauding nomads. Gideon protested that God must have the wrong man. But when the angel caused fire to burst from a rock, Gideon decided that God was a better military strategist than he, and began recruiting troops.

The Midianites, massed in a nearby valley, were 135,000 strong, outnumbering the Hebrews four to one. Yet God ordered Gideon to send home all but his bravest soldiers.

Next God told Gideon to lead his men to the river. "Send away any who kneel and drink directly from the river, rather than lapping water from their hands," He commanded.

Gideon was steadfast enough to obey the Lord's directives, but still, when he found himself left with only 300 men, he was nervous. So that night, God had him sneak down to the Midianite camp. There he heard an enemy guard describing his dream, in which a cake of barley bread had tumbled into the Midianite camp, flattening it. "This is a sign that Gideon's forces will defeat us," responded a second guard.

His confidence bolstered by what he'd heard, Gideon returned to his own camp, awoke his men, and directed them to spread out around the Midianites, armed with trumpets, torches, and clay jars for covering their lights. Thus Gideon's small army crept up on and encircled its sleeping enemy.

Then Gideon blew his trumpet, long and loud, and smashed his jar, allowing his torch's light to blaze forth. His men followed his shining example. The sudden blares and glares awoke the Midianites. Those who didn't flee in terror were so confused they turned their swords on one another.

Israelite reinforcements arrived and clinched Gideon's victory. And Gideon learned that with God on his side, he could accomplish the impossible.

THE BATTLE AT FINGER LAKE
Lawrence E. Wilson

We called it "Arizona" but it was far from home. Southwest of Danang, this area of South Vietnam was suspected of being heavily infested with enemy forces. On November 21, 1967, my men and I were participating in a sweep of the northeastern corner of Arizona Territory. Our mission was to destroy or capture the enemy and their supplies. Moving on line, side by side, through the cover of the trees at the foot of Finger Lake, we had worked our way halfway up the west side of the lake. There, at a bend in the lake, we discovered a small village, completely deserted.

It was lunchtime, and my radioman and I took shelter in a well-constructed cement-block hooch. A lazy breeze stirred the broad leaves of the surrounding trees and, as I grabbed a bite of chow, I thought how peaceful the spot seemed. I was grateful that my men were getting a rest. Still, concerns about the whereabouts of the enemy gnawed at my mind and I was glad I had a couple of listening posts deployed, hidden in some shrubbery 25 yards beyond the front of our line.

I was a lieutenant in the Marine Corps, in command of the 35 men of the First Platoon, India Company. The Second Platoon was also in the general area and, after we had eaten, I called the leader of that platoon to coordinate: "India 2, we're about ready to head out here. How 'bout we lead, and you follow?"

"Sounds good to me," he said, and I passed the word to my men to saddle up.

I stood up, and the serenity of the setting was shattered by the fierce staccato of a machine gun, punctuated by massive fire from small arms. Bullets pierced the thatched roof of the hooch, exploding all around us as they slapped into the walls and dirt.

Instantly the air was filled with the shrieks of men who had been hit, and urgent cries of "Corpsman!"

My heart pounded in terror, and my brain was racing: *Where was the enemy and how could I counter them?* But as I tried to analyze the situation, the incoming fire intensified. Mortar shells began thudding into the roofs and treetops around us. Alarmed, I radioed the Company Commander, over on the east side of the lake, for assistance. "We're in very deep trouble here," I told him, panic obvious in my voice.

"Calm down, Lieutenant," the Commander said patronizingly. "We'll get to you as soon as we can." I couldn't seem to convince him that we were experiencing an extraordinarily violent attack. Looking back, I think he was still operating on an earlier premise that he was in a position to encounter the main force of the enemy, and that I had just encountered a small diversionary force.

For the time being, it seemed, we were on our own. I did not even have access to the controllers who would normally arrange for artillery backup and air support, as they were with the Company Commander. And the enemy was beginning to overrun us. Fortunately, one of my machine gunners had already set up and was effectively holding off some of them. But it was up to me to find ways to move my men into an advantageous position, pour on more firepower, and put the enemy on the defensive.

First I needed to get a better idea of the enemy's location. Leaving the safety of the hooch, I moved to a rise next to an old bomb crater, on the edge of a rice paddy. The enemy spotted me and started spraying bullets in my direction; but at least now I could pinpoint the enemy position, at the base of the tree line along Finger Lake, about 50 meters across the paddy to our front. I could see a heavy machine gun firing at us from this tree line.

At this moment, one of my corpsmen, "Doc Mac," sprinted up to me. "PFC O'Neil has taken a machine-gun blast in the chest,"

CARRYING WATER

We had in the Twenty-third Ohio (Hayes' Regiment) a quaint old character—an enlisted musician—whose name I would not mention for anything. Just before the battle of South Mountain he came to me and asked me to step aside with him a moment. I did so, and he said: "My God, Major, I am a coward! I did not know it. I thought I could help the country, and, though I was past 45 and needn't to, I enlisted. Now I have found that I can't go into a fight! I can't, Major, if you should kill me! I shall be disgraced, and all the folks back home will know it. I can never hold my head up again if I try to go into this fight. Can't you do something for me? Give me something to do that ain't fighting and I'll do anything. Oh, for God's sake, Major, think of something and save me from the disgrace!"

The poor fellow was half frantic in his earnestness. I thought a moment and said: "A, do you think you could carry water for the men while they are fighting? It is going to be an awful hot day and a canteen of fresh water will be about the greatest luxury the men could have under fire. Can you carry water for them?" "Oh, yes. Thank you, Major." Well, now, in the thickest of that fight, where the regiment lost within eight men of half that went into action, old A would come to the front loaded down with canteens, delivering them, and taking up the empty ones along the line. Between bayonet charges the men were hugging the ground like a long-lost brother, under such a storm of minie balls as did not seem to leave any occupied space in the air. Old A would prance down the line delivering canteens to the panting men without any more sense of fear than the bravest man in the army, until his last canteen of water was gone, then he would give a wild yell and bolt for the rear as if the devil was after him.—Brigadier General Comly

This account comes from Civil War Scrapbooks, Vol. 13, in the Ohio Historical Society Collections, Columbus, Ohio.

he screamed frantically. "His lungs are falling out of his back, and I've wrapped tape around his torso to try and keep them in, but I don't know how long I can keep him alive. You've gotta get him out of here," he pleaded.

Turning my attention momentarily from problems of strategy, I designated an area behind me for staging the wounded and medical evacuations. "Art, get on the horn and call in a priority medivac, now!" I yelled to my radioman.

Everything was happening at once. I returned my focus to the problem of increasing our fire superiority. It would be highly irregular for a platoon commander to make direct contact with our artillery battery, but I couldn't allow my men to be slaughtered. Using one of the two handsets I was holding, I radioed our artillery battery and arranged for them to begin shelling the enemy from their location on a hill outside Arizona Territory.

In the middle of coordinating the artillery assault, I looked over my shoulder and caught my Weapons Team Leader's attention. "Get the rocket team up here," I yelled, pointing to a bomb crater to my right. When they arrived I'd have them zero in on the enemy machine-gun location I'd spotted.

Now for air support. Fortunately an independent airborne Air Controller had heard our appeal for a medivac chopper and contacted us to see what assistance he could offer. Over the medivac frequency on my other handset, I advised him of the locations of the enemy and friendly forces.

"The enemy's too close for regular bombs," he stated. "I can get napalm in—there's some Air Force Phantoms heading down from the north that had to abort a bombing run. But I have to warn you, some of your Marines might get hit. Your call."

There seemed to be no alternative—with our casualties mounting, the enemy was on the verge of overwhelming us. Through the Controller, I vectored the Phantoms in. By now, my rocket team was ready to fire. Our first target was the enemy machine gun. A rocket projectile and a load of napalm hit the machine gun at the same time, wiping it out.

The jets made several runs to drop napalm as I held my breath and prayed for my men's safety. Luckily none of my men was hit. Now I felt it was time for us to make our first counterassault. Discovering that the jets had 20-millimeter cannon available, I asked the Controller to have them make a cannon run on the enemy.

Two aircraft came in, one after the other, blasting bullets the size of cucumbers. The deafening noise was as deep and heavy as a foghorn. "Give me another pass, so we can maneuver closer," I asked the controller but, to my dismay, he told me the jets had used up all their cannon rounds. What now? Thinking quickly, I came up with a plan. If the jets made another run "dry," the enemy would have their heads down to protect themselves against the expected cannon bursts, and we could charge them while the jets were flying in, knowing that the cannons wouldn't be firing.

There was just time to give my men the order to assault. "Go now!" I hollered, as the jets bore down. My men's faces told me they thought I must be crazy, asking them to put themselves out in the open, for they did not know that the jets would not be firing. But, God bless them, they put their faith in me. As the jets passed, my Marines got up, one after the other, and courageously charged the tree line, routing the enemy. They even retrieved two of our men who, unbeknownst to me, had been dragged away when the enemy overran us.

Their assault drove the enemy farther up the left side of Finger Lake and out into a rice paddy, and the Forward Air Controller called in another flight of jets to continue the attack. After the last run, he counted approximately 80 enemy killed.

By now we had been fighting four or five hours. Thinking the battle was over, I regrouped my platoon and called in a medivac chopper. Finally I'd be able to get some help for PFC O'Neil and my other wounded men. But as the helicopter got within a few feet of touching down, bullets suddenly riddled it.

I was astounded and disheartened to find that after all the fighting and air strikes, we still had enemy attacking us. Where were they coming from? Every time we beat them back, they reappeared, as strong as ever. This new attack seemed to be directed from a hooch surrounded by trees, across the open rice paddy to our left.

The Forward Air Controller had long since departed the area, but luckily a U. S. Army Huey gunship came up on the medivac frequency and offered his assistance. Grateful for his offer, I attempted to vector him to the hooch, but he just couldn't see it.

I called for one of my most experienced Marines. "Take some men and mark that hooch with smoke," I directed him. Thirty minutes later, we saw a yellow plume rising from an area of rice paddy to the right of the hooch. Corporal Dumont had hit his target with the smoke grenade.

Now I was able to vector in the helicopter more precisely. Within minutes, the pilot had the hooch in sight and unloaded on it, destroying the enemy inside.

Time to try another medical evacuation. When the chopper came in, my heart was in my throat; however, the medivac went off without a hitch. Finally, we had finished, I thought to myself with a sigh of relief.

But, to my dismay, I began receiving reports from my men in the tree line that they were hearing yet another buildup of enemy forces to their front. In the gathering twilight, the enemy began to taunt us, calling out, "Marine, you die tonight."

Casualties had reduced my platoon to almost one-third its

original size. I was sure we would be overrun during the night and began to formulate a survival plan: I would have to pull in our perimeter and call in the Second Platoon; we could use tear gas to try and hold the enemy at bay. I didn't allow myself to ponder the thought that we probably wouldn't make it through the night.

At this point, I received a call from the Company Commander, the first since the battle had begun. He was unable to get to us because of enemy forces between his position and ours but he could have reinforcements flown in "if you still feel you need them."

Within the hour, we heard the welcome drone of a large number of helicopters coming toward us from the paddy to our left. As they landed and Marines disembarked in full battle dress, ready to fight, our hearts pounded with joy, pride and relief. With fresh reinforcements, we survived and defeated the enemy and went on to fight more battles.

The next morning, we received replacements for our casualties. All but 12 of my men had received serious wounds. To my great sorrow, two of them had been killed. PFC O'Neil didn't make it and PFC Charles N. Taylor III died of a bullet wound to the head.

The estimated enemy force was 300. An extensive tunnel complex was discovered, leading into the area where the enemy chose to stand and fight, and we believe that this tunnel system enabled them to keep reinforcing their forces, despite extensive battle casualties.

The day after the battle, the Battalion Commander came out to Finger Lake to assess the operation and present Purple Heart Medals to the wounded men of the First Platoon who had not been evacuated. I heard him ask our Company Commander what had happened at Finger Lake the previous day and heard the

Company Commander respond dismissively, "Oh, you mean Larry's little thing?" I felt as if I'd been slapped in the face.

I never received any recognition from my superiors for my actions at Finger Lake, but several months later I found out that my men had put me in for the Bronze Star Medal, in recognition of my efforts to keep them alive that day. I received the award, and it remains one of my most treasured accolades.

But for years I wondered if my commander had been right and that if the battle was, indeed, nothing to write home about. As time has passed and I have talked with others, however, I have realized that for six hellish hours, my men and I fought a very significant battle.

Every Marine fighting that day performed heroically, and each and every one of them deserves commendation. I therefore dedicate this record to them, as my way of recognizing their courage and tenacity and the importance of their actions: YOU SHOULD HAVE SEEN HOW WELL MY MEN FOUGHT!

Larry Wilson served in the Marine Corps from 1966 to 1969. He became an FBI special agent, retiring in 1994, and is now an investigative consultant. He lives in California and Newfoundland.

> *"Life has meaning only in the struggles.*
> *Triumph or defeat is in the hands of the Gods.*
> *So let us celebrate the struggles."*
> —Swahili warrior song

DEATH WAS OUR ESCORT
Ernest G. Vetter
(as told to him by Lt. j.g. Edward T. Hamilton, USNR)

Editor's Note: *Patrol Torpedo boats, PT boats for short, were small attack craft used extensively by the U.S. in World War II. Known collectively as the Mosquito Fleet, these fragile plywood cockleshells were built for speed and held a crew of twelve. This is the story of one PT boat mission out of New Guinea.*

We had been operating from Porlock for about two months. Action had hardened and toughened us. It had a different effect on the boats. They'd taken on a lot of lead; the engines needed overhauling, and we didn't have many screws left that hadn't been chewed to pieces by the coral. Only four of our craft were still operating.

We were tough but tired. It seemed about time for some relief to come. It was just at this stage that Barnes got a radio message from Milne Bay headquarters asking us to do a job that would have been difficult even for fresh men and new boats. The message said that a Japanese troop transport, trying to sneak through our waters under cover of darkness, had piled up on a reef in our territory. She was just out of reach of Army artillery and carried so much antiaircraft that bombers couldn't get below 20,000 feet. Would we blow her up? And, the message finished, would we be so kind as to use only one torpedo, as they were very hard to get?

"How do you like that?" Barnes snorted. "Use only one torpedo! They're hard to get! A boat with so many guns aboard her the bombers can't come down, and we're supposed to run up politely and plug her with just one shot!"

"Do they count duds?" I asked. We'd been having a lot of them lately. "Or do we get a free shot if the fish doesn't go off?"

Barnes looked at me reflectively for a moment. "Shotgun," he said, "you don't look so good. You've been out every night lately. Why don't you stay behind tonight and get a little rest? I'll handle this job."

I knew what Barnes was thinking. His idea was that this was about the most dangerous job yet and it wouldn't do any good for both of us to be knocked off at the same time. So he was going to take the risk. He was right about not risking any more officers than was necessary, but I couldn't let him go off alone. I think Barnes was pleased when I refused. We were a good team and liked to go out together. I felt safer when he was along and I think he felt the same way about me.

None of the men was very cheerful when we started out that night. We knew the risks were high. The reward was high, too—a big transport choked with troops. If we could destroy it, even if we were lost ourselves, that would be a big gain for our side. The operation had to be undertaken even if the odds were against us. We were willing to take the short end of the gamble because of the size of the stake but we still didn't feel good about it. The deep dark thoughts turned and turned within us as we sailed out through the night, knowing that this might be the last time we would see this harbor, which somehow had suddenly become an attractive spot, a place to which we wanted to come back

It was 1:45 in the morning when we spotted our objective—a tremendous dark blur rising up out of the water. All talking stopped. Our engines were held down to their lowest possible speed, so we could move in as silently as possible. We were all but drifting in, ready at a second's notice to drop the mufflers and roar forward at full speed.

We crept up to within 400 yards. Still the transport slumbered. Three hundred. No signs of life. Now we were near enough

> *"Courage is like love; it must have hope to nourish it."*
> —Napoleon Bonaparte

to be sure of our result. Ordinarily, we would have launched at least two torpedoes to guard against a miss or a dud. If we fired only one and it didn't explode, the ship would be warned; and instead of losing one torpedo, the Navy might lose four torpedoes, one PT boat and fourteen men. Perhaps that was a calculation the mathematicians at Milne Bay had forgotten to make.

We had our orders and we obeyed them. We fired a single torpedo and watched its wake streak across the water in a perfect straight line to the target. It was a beautiful hit, smack on number three hold. It was a dud!

Now we were in for it. The impact on the ship's hull could be heard clearly across the 300 yards of water that separated us from the transport. The general alarm sounded on the ship. Searchlights were switched on, sweeping the water to find us. We fired a second torpedo. It hit the transport midships—and it was another dud!

Bower was frantic."We can't get enough torpedoes," he wailed. "And the ones we do get won't go off! Shall I fire three, Captain? I know this one'll work! This one has to work!"

Monroe glanced questioningly at Barnes. He had already committed a technical violation of instructions in firing this second torpedo—if Milne Bay counted duds. What else could we do?

Torpedo three leapt from the tube, ran straight out a few yards, turned, and headed straight for us.

At the same moment, the first Jap searchlight found us and we were immediately caught in a hail of bullets.

Everything seemed to be happening at once. I let out a yell as

> *"Never, never, never, never give up."*
> —Winston Churchill

the torpedo swung at us. Monroe took in the situation at a glance. We were on a double spot. We might be annihilated either by Jap gunfire or our own torpedo.

Monroe saw he didn't have time to turn. There was only one way to go, the way we were headed—toward the Jap ship. He shot us forward, straight into the Jap fire, missing the torpedo by inches with a desperate swerve that slowed us up and brought us close to the transport.

The gunners on the Jap ship had been confused when we came in toward them, the one direction they hadn't expected us to take. But they were swinging their guns toward us and we were so near that they would blow us out of the water unless we got away fast enough. Monroe turned the boat in a hairpin curve and, as he did, he yelled: "Prepare to fire 180 degrees to the rear!"

Bower sprang to the torpedo tube to set the tin fish for the difficult shot backwards. It was our last torpedo. Was it defective, like the first three?

"Ready to fire!" he shouted.

The boat was picking up speed as she completed her turn, leaving a foaming arc behind her on the dark water. Meanwhile, Monroe gazed backwards as he steered, carefully watching our wake. The curving line of foam speeding from our stern straightened out. This was the moment for which Monroe had been waiting. He sighted along the line of the wake and pressed the firing button.

The torpedo plunged from the tube, traveling away from the

target and, for a second, as we overtook it, ran parallel to PT 120. Then its gyro took hold. The torpedo described a half circle and streaked straight back toward the enemy ship. As we ran from the pursuing bullets, we could see the white line of foam lengthen across the water. It seemed to be headed right, but as we drew farther away we lost it. We held our breaths.

And then it came! There was a terrific explosion. Flames sprang up instantaneously from the decks of the ship. We had scored a hit!

We swung around and went in again. Some of the transport's guns were still firing; some had stopped. Again and again, we roared by, pouring lead into the ship until all firing had ceased, either because we had gotten the gunners or because they had to join the fire fighters. When the shooting stopped, we turned and made for home, leaving the fire to finish our work.

NOMS DE GUERRE

In the Middle Ages, a lion was a symbol for courage and fortitude. The 12th-century English king and crusader, whose exploits in battle were celebrated in minstrels' lyrics became known as Richard the Lion-Hearted. His contemporary, Richard de Clare, Earl of Pembroke, was dubbed Strongbow by his men, in tribute to his skill in Irish campaigns.

American military heroes include Old Hickory, the name given to future U.S. President Andrew Jackson, who commanded a troop of 2,000 Tennessee volunteers during the War of 1812. After following orders to march his troops to Natchez, Jackson waited around for weeks, only to be told to dismiss his soldiers. They were 500 miles from home and many of the men were sick, but the U.S. Army furnished no provisions for the return trip. The concerned Jackson advanced the money for supplies out of his own pocket. Furthermore, in order that ill foot soldiers might go on horseback, he ordered his officers to walk and he did likewise. Impressed by their leader's strength in sharing their hardships, his men gave him a nickname that implies he was as tough as hickory wood.

Another revealing nickname was Bloody Arm, the appellation earned by freed slave Jim Beckwourth, who became a legendary Rocky Mountain fur trapper and explorer as well as a warrior who fought alongside the Crow Indians. Bloody Arm was known both for his valor on the battlefield and his courage in facing down dangerous animals. He once took on a grizzly bear that had been terrorizing a Crow village. The grizzly had already killed two children and a strong young brave when Beckwourth entered its cave, armed with a knife. Beckwourth emerged victorious. However, his arm was badly injured, giving rise to the honorific "Bloody Arm," an expression of the Crows' respect.

THIS WAS MY BEST, THAT DAY

Dear Mom,

I held him in my arms like a father

holding his newborn son, proud and afraid.

I was afraid that he would die

before I had a chance

to tell him

what he needed to hear.

He looked up at me and smiled,

trusting me,

believing in my strength and courage;

believing that I could carry him to safety.

I lied to him.

I told him fairy tales,

stories I heard as a child.

He looked at me

and listened,

his eyes filled with wonder and hope.

He was innocent and pure,

a child cradled in the arms of weakness

and doubt,

swaddled in trembling fear and desperation.

His eyes closed slowly,

and his arm slipped off my shoulder.

It hung limp and lifeless at my side.

His body,

draped over my arms like a green shroud,

relaxed and rested,

shed its *bone-tired* weariness

and final fear.

He was asleep,

peaceful, eternal sleep.

He was no longer troubled by the thoughts of war

—the fear of death.

I laid him on the ground in a soft bed

of blood red dirt.

I removed my flak jacket and placed it

under his head for comfort.

I pulled a canteen from a pouch on my web belt,

unscrewed the cap

and poured some over my fingers.

I touched his eyes, hands and boots

with my wet fingers;

and mumbled this simple prayer:

I give up

to You,

this innocent child,

God!

My arms are tired.

He is too heavy

for me to carry.

Forgive this man

and take him

to his final resting place

beside You.

I scooped up a handful of dirt
and sprinkled it over his body,
burying him deep
in my memory.

Like me,
Mom,
he is just eighteen,
alone
and frightened
—and afraid
of dying.

That fear is over.

A voice called.
I picked up my rifle
and ran for cover.

This was my best
that day,
Mom.

Your son,
Private First Class L. Parrillo, USMC 1/1
Vietnam 1969

While serving as a Marine, Louis Parrillo attained the rank of Lance Corporal. Wounded in a firefight in Vietnam, he was hospitalized and in a body cast for eight months. After discharge, he lived in Norton, Ohio, where he worked as a carpenter. He died in 1990.

SECTION VI

◆ DEGREES OF KNOWLEDGE ◆

*"I have learned that success is to be measured
not so much by the position that one has
reached in life as by the obstacles which he has
overcome while trying to succeed."*

—BOOKER T. WASHINGTON

YES AND NO
Ellyn Houston

I gnoring the burning red welt on my arm, I focused on the 12-year-old sitting innocently across from me. She continued stringing beads with autistic concentration. During my year as a special ed assistant in a south Montana grade school, I'd learned that repetition was key to success with this child. I restated my directive: "Brittney, it's time to put away the beads."

Brittney tweaked my arm again, hard, and recited a familiar babble of syllables, "Jah da ha pich." So, now I was a b—ch. Brit's vocabulary was limited yet diversified.

What now? I asked myself. Mercifully, Brittney's attention was drawn to her classmates setting out glasses and napkins for snack, and she began asking, with the mechanical repetitiveness of a metronome, "Nummies? Nummies? Nummies?"

Insistent, I replied, "First we pick up the beads, then we go yuck, then nummies."

"Yuck," Brittney acknowledged, folding her right hand to sign the letter "T," for toilet, and shaking it in my direction.

Pointing to the beads, I reminded her, "First this, then you go yuck."

Brit sealed the beads in the tin, made her toilet visit and returned to the table as Lil, my co-teacher, passed out treats. Placing the fingertips of her right hand in her upturned left palm, Lil pantomimed twisting apart an Oreo. "Brit, do you want a cookie . . ."

"Yes," Brit interrupted.

Lil continued, tapping her left elbow with the thumb side of her right fist. "Or do you want a cracker?"

"Yes."

Lil looked at me for direction. I shrugged my shoulders to indicate that I hadn't a clue. "Try a cookie," I ventured.

Brit took a bite of the cookie Lil offered. "Guck!" she exclaimed, and then froze, afraid any movement would allow the cookie to pass further beyond her lips. In an effort to rid herself of the repugnant substance, she leaned forward, allowing cookie and spittle to drip to the table.

I wiped Brittany's fingers and mouth with paper towels. "Guess we'd better try a cracker instead."

This offering met with Brit's approval, and she licked off the cheese spread and munched the cracker into oblivion. As she finished her snack I packed her backpack for the bus ride home.

After the children had left, I squeezed my frame into a child-sized desk. "It's going to be a long year if Brittney doesn't learn to say no," I sighed.

Lil, seated at her desk, looked up from the lesson plan she was working on. "At least she's learned that saying yes gets a response."

"But the response isn't always what she's expecting," I lamented.

Because Brittney required fulltime one-on-one attention, teaching her was my primary job responsibility. I was aware that I would need patience to teach Brit to use yes and no appropriately. Patience, and a good strategy. I called Diana, Brittney's mother. "I'm trying to teach Brit a new skill," I explained, "and I know food is her favorite incentive. Would it be okay if I add some new items to Brittney's diet at school?" Diana gave her permission gladly.

Early the next day, I collected a box containing glue, paper clips, tape, pens, pencils, and chalk, which I placed at the end of a table. Next to it, I placed a bag of raisins and a box of cereal. "Nummies?" Brit immediately questioned, noticing the food as she sat down.

I held out a raisin. "Do you want this?"

"Yes."

I gave her the raisin and, when she had finished chewing, I held out another. "Brittney, do you want this?"

"Yes."

I picked up a glue bottle and asked, "Brittney, do you want this?"

"Yes." She grabbed the bottle and stuck the orange tip in her mouth. "Guck."

"You're right, Brit, that is a guck." Taking her head in my hands, I shook it back and forth. "You don't want that. No-o-o." I took the glue bottle.

"Yes," said Brittney.

Promptly giving the bottle back, I asked, "Is that what you want?"

She stared at the bottle, confused. "No," I prompted her. "You don't want that. Tell me 'No.' " I shook my head with slow exaggeration. Then I offered a piece of cereal. "Brit, do you want this?"

She laid down the glue and took the cereal. "Yes." Throughout the day she tasted raisins, cereal, chalk, pens, and pencils, as I repeated the lesson again and again.

The following morning, I was anxious to see what Brittney had retained. "Nummies?" she asked as soon as she stepped off the bus. Inside, Brit sat at the table, anxious to start. "Nummies? Nummies?"

I held out a raisin. "Brit, do you want this?"

"Yes." She popped the raisin in her mouth and chewed. "Guck." Raisin pulp oozed to the table below.

Putting my chin in my hand, I inhaled deeply, then exhaled audibly as I observed Brittney through the two fingers propped under my eyebrow. *Patience*, I told myself, *patience.*

But as days turned into weeks, I began to doubt my ability to teach Brittney to use no. In my moments of discouragement, I

FACING THE FROG: *A PHILOSOPHICAL VIEW*

Fortitude is the guard and support of the other virtues . . .The first step to get this noble and manly steadiness is carefully to keep children from frights of all kinds when they are young . . .The next thing is by gentle degrees to accustom children to those things they are too much afraid of. . .Your child shrieks, and runs away at the sight of a frog; let  another catch it, and lay it down at a good distance from him: at first accustom him to look upon it; when he can do that, then to come nearer to it, and see it leap without emotion; then to touch it lightly, when it is held fast in another's hand; and so on, till he can come to handle it as confidently as a butterfly or a sparrow . . . Successes of this kind, often repeated, will make him find that evils are not always so certain or so great as our fears represent them; and that the way to avoid them is not to run away." —John Locke, *Some Thoughts Concerning Education,* 1692

would remind myself of all the times in the past Brittney had proved to me she could learn new things. Don't give up on her, I would think, fortifying myself for another round of frustration.

Summer gave way to autumn, and suddenly, it was the end of October. Vampires, princesses and clowns paraded down the hall. Brittney, dressed as a surgeon, sat on the floor, spinning around on her bottom. I took her hand and led her back to the table. "Come on, Nellie, it's time to do some work." Brittney retorted with a grunt, and I laughed. "You don't like being called Nellie?" Another snort. "Well," I responded teasingly, "what if I want to call you Nellie, Nellie?"

Brit made perfect eye contact, her mouth pursed in a tight smile. Lips slowly unzipping , she growled, "B—ch."

Unable to maintain my usual response of ignoring her, I laughed. I handed her the frames of some puzzles but kept the puzzle pieces out of her reach. Offering her a Halloween candy, I asked, "Do you want this?"

"Yes."

As she chewed the candy, I held up a puzzle piece. "Brit, do you want this?" She tried taking the piece without answering. I held it tight. "Use your words, Brit. Do you want this?"

"Yes." I gave her the piece, and she added it to the frame.

Alternating between candy and puzzle pieces, she chewed and fit puzzles together. Finally, I held out a pencil. "Brit, do you want this?"

Then it happened. Chestnut brown curls shimmied as she vigorously shook her head. "No, no, nos," she said.

"Nice talking, Brit!" Dying to hug her, but not wanting to break our rhythm, I held up another puzzle piece. "Brit, do you want this?"

"Yes." She took the piece and placed it in the appropriate vacancy.

I grabbed a pen. "Brit, do you want this?"

"No, no, nos."

"Brit, do you want hugs?"

"Yes."

As she crawled on my lap, I wrapped my arms around her and crooned, "Who's a smart girl?"

"Mes." she said, adding the familiar "s" and patting her chest.

"That's right. Who's a pretty girl?"

"Mes."

"That's right."

Throughout the rest of the school year, Brit practiced her new skill, enjoying the power that comes with using yes and no correctly. That March I gave notice to the school district that I would be resigning. I trained my replacement for two weeks, hoping this would make the transition easier for Brit.

I had requested permission from Diana to take Brit out the evening of our last day together. As I knocked at the door that evening, I heard Diana say, "Brit, go see who's here." Brittney opened the door a crack and peeked out. Seeing me, she opened the door wide and wrapped her arms around my neck. "Yes," she said and took my hand to lead me inside.

Diana sat at the kitchen table. "Brit, it's time for your meds."

"No, no, nos." Leaving me with her mom, Brit walked into the living room, plopped in front of a stereo speaker, and began listening to country music.

Diana turned to me, grinning. "You know, some days I hate you for that."

After we left the house, Brit and I stopped at a pizza parlor for dinner. While we awaited our pepperoni pizza, I led Brit to the salad bar. "Do you want tomatoes, Brit?" "Yes." "Do you want green pepper?" "No, no, nos." She returned to our table with a variety of vegetables and fruit. No raisins.

Back in the car, heading to her house, I turned on the radio. "Hey, Brit, how about some tunes?"

"Yes."

As the Beach Boys extolled vacation hot spots from Aruba to Key Largo, I swayed my shoulders in rhythm with the melody. "Sorry, girl, no country and western in this car," I said.

Brit stared out the window. But the sly grin on her face was apparent even in profile; and I heard her mutter dismissively, "Geek."

A social worker for 15 years, Ellyn Houston recently became a first-time mom and has embarked on a new career as a writer. She lives with her husband and son in southwest Georgia.

HOW INTEGRATION CAME TO ONE MISSISSIPPI TOWN

In August of 1965, in the heart of the Mississippi Delta, seven brothers and sisters registered for school in the tiny town of Drew. Their parents were Mae Bertha and Matthew Carter, poor black cotton sharecroppers, who were taking advantage of a new law that allowed them to enroll their children in previously all-white schools. The Carters didn't realize that they were the only black family in all of Sunflower County taking this bold step. All they knew was that their children were not getting the education they would need to escape the cotton fields. As Mae Bertha told it, "I was tired of my kids coming home with pages torn out of worn-out books that came from the white school. I was tired of them riding on old raggedy buses after the white children didn't want to ride on them anymore. I was just tired."

The Civil Rights Act of 1964 had ordered the desegregation of all public schools receiving federal aid. In response, many southern school districts—Drew's included—had drawn up "freedom of choice" plans, authorizing parents to send their children to the schools of their choice. But most school boards were confident that their plans would lie fallow. White community leaders knew that rural blacks were dependent on whites for work and housing, and most would not dare alienate the "boss" community by choosing "white" schools for their children.

The Carters dared. But no sooner had they enrolled their children in the Drew schools than Mr. Thornton, the overseer of the plantation where they "cropped," paid Matthew a visit to persuade him to "withdraw the children out." Mae Bertha, overhearing the men's conversation, fetched a record player from the house, set it up on the porch, and turned the volume way up high, playing a speech by John. F Kennedy: "When Americans are sent to Vietnam or West Berlin, we do not ask for whites only. It ought to be possible, therefore, for American students of any color to attend any public institution."

Soon afterward Matthew Carter was wakened at 3:00 a.m. by the crunch of gravel. Gunshots rang out, followed by a squeal of tires as cars sped away. Matthew quickly made a check of his family. No one was hurt—but several bullet holes marked the wall above the bed where two of the children had been sleeping.

The Carters held firm. The first day of school, their children were on the school bus bound for Drew. "Go back to your own schools, niggers," shouted white hecklers standing along the streets of town. As 16-year-old Ruth Carter descended from the bus, she was scared but took heart from her mother's words: "That school is not white, it's brown brick, and that school belongs to you as well as it belongs to the white children."

Back at home, Mae Bertha, sick with anxiety, prayed and fortified herself with the message of a preacher she had once heard: "Everybody's afraid and it's okay to be afraid, but you can't let it stop you."

The local store cut off the Carters' credit. One moonless night, someone set loose their cows and pigs, which were never seen again. The plantation overseer announced he had no land for Matthew to work and that the family would have to move. But the Carter children stayed in the Drew schools.

For five years, until the courts ordered complete desegregation in 1970, the Carter children endured name-calling, spitballs, social isolation. But rarely did any of them speak of quitting. Gloria, a seventh-grader in 1965, reports, "I kept saying to myself, 'We are not going to let 'em run us away.' "

Eight Carter children eventually graduated from Drew High.

On the University of Mississippi campus there is an area called "The Circle," where riots errupted in 1962 when James Meredith attempted to integrate the university. On October 2, 1999, in The Circle, a small Japanese magnolia with two purple blossoms was planted. Beneath the tree, the plaque reads:

In memoriam: Mae Bertha Carter
January 13, 1923 - April 28, 1999
Mother of Seven Ole Miss graduates
—Constance Curry

Constance Curry wrote about the Carter family in Silver Rights *(Algonquin Books, 1995). Her newest book is* The Fire Ever Burning *(University Press of Mississippi, 2000).*

GEORGE PATTON AND ME
Girard Sagmiller

rowing up in North Dakota, I loved to listen to my dad's World War II stories, perhaps as much as he loved to tell them. Many a Sunday after church, my stomach pleasantly full of roast beef or fried chicken, I would sit back in my chair at the round oak table in our dining room, ready to be transported into a world of heroes. Often the stories were about General George Patton, my father's idol. "General Patton was a great general and a great American," Dad would intone, reliving the time when as a soldier he had actually seen Patton. "As he passed by in his jeep, he seemed bigger than life. You could see the confidence shining in his face. And you could tell he was determined to do whatever it took to win the war."

I wanted to be just like General Patton. Playing war with the neighborhood kids, armed with snowball artillery, I would strike a commanding pose atop a hill of snow, a glint of assurance in my eyes, imagining that I was a great general, about to lead my troops forward to overtake the enemy. But the pride I felt on this pretend battlefield was a fleeting emotion, one I rarely experienced outside of play.

For I had dyslexia—a learning disability that made it hard for me to read and write. At school, I was engaged in my own private war, one where victories were few. No matter how hard I tried, I couldn't seem to catch on to the things that came so easily to other students.

Every day I would be banished from class for special reading instruction. I watched the second hand circling the clock at the front of the classroom, hoping that for once, the teacher would forget to dismiss me, dreading the moment when she would announce, "Will the slower readers please join Mrs. White in the hall outside the classroom." Rising from my seat, I would steel myself to ignore the whispered potshots of other children: "Hey stupid, time for your idiot class." "Will all the *dummies* meet Mrs. White outside?"

Hanging my head in shame, I walked slowly down the aisle to join other members of the special group, as the teacher paused in her lesson, awaiting our departure. The other special students and I followed our reading teacher toward the janitor's storage room, the only space available for us, where we would meet amidst mops and brooms in an atmosphere pervaded by the smell of cleaning fluid. As we trooped down the hall, we maintained an eerie silence, hoping not to attract attention from children in other classes.

The best method for teaching dyslexic individuals to read is phonics, helping them link the letters on a page with sounds. But phonics was out of fashion in my school. Instead, throughout the years, my special ed teachers experimented with the latest flashcards, slides and games in an effort to find the magical teaching tool that would help me perform like the rest of the class. One year I was even given a special desk, placed to one side of the regular classroom. The desk was surrounded by walls so high that I could neither see out nor be seen as I listened to tapes drilling me in subjects like grammar and spelling. "See, Girard, isn't this nice?" said the teacher enthusiastically. " You've got your own private study nook to help you concentrate and not be distracted." But the teacher's sales pitch did nothing to soften the humiliation I felt at being isolated like a P.O.W.

Some teachers just viewed me as stupid, lazy and inconvenient. The worst of these was one student-teacher assigned to my reading group. This teacher, his face pinched into a scowl, sometimes grew so frustrated with our reading difficulties that he would grab one of us from a chair and shake him.

One day, at my turn to read, I encountered a word I could not decipher, no matter how hard I tried. The student-teacher, already inflamed by the mistakes of another student, began pounding his fists on my desk, and then grabbed my shoulders, yelling at the top of his voice, "You are going to read that word! You don't want to know what's going to happen if you don't!" My heart was pounding, and tears began streaming down my face. I bent my head to my book and tried again to read the word, but it was no use.

Letting go of my shoulders, the teacher strode over to his desk and picked up a pair of scissors. "One last time. What is that word, Girard?" he demanded as he returned to tower over me, grasping the scissors like a knife. I tried again. Again I failed. A streak of silver flashed through the air toward my desk. I jerked my hand away, and the scissors in my teacher's hand lodged in the desktop where my own hand had been only seconds before.

Releasing the scissors, my teacher lifted me violently out of my seat, holding me eye-to-eye with him, two feet in the air. I heard my shirt rip and felt an unlaced shoe drop from my foot. "Now look what you made me do!" he barked accusingly. Then he threw me back into my seat, kicked open the door, and stalked out.

Luckily, when I returned to my regular classroom, the teacher there spotted my torn shirt and tear-stained face, and persuaded me to tell her what had happened. As a result, the teacher who had attacked me was never allowed to teach again. But the damage to my self-esteem and sense of safety had already been done. More than ever, I looked at school as a war zone.

Every afternoon, I returned home from school feeling I had lost another battle. Every evening, I took my dad's war book from the bookshelf and turned straight to the picture of General Patton. How I wished he would come alive from the pages and lead me to victory. How I wished I could be like him, strong, fearless and triumphant. And then my hopeless tears would begin. "You'll never be like him, with your dumb old dyslexia," I told myself. I could never even be fit for his command, wounded as I already was.

I learned to pretend that I didn't care about grades, and graduated from high school by the skin of my teeth. College seemed out of the question. I found my way into the military, serving for seven years with the National Guard Army. And there I learned that I *am* like General Patton.

One commanding officer was an army history buff, and one day we were talking about Patton. "Helluva guy, Patton," my CO said. Then he dropped a bombshell. "Did you know he was dyslexic?" My face registered shock, and the CO continued his history lesson. "He had an awful time in school when he was a kid because reading and writing were so hard for him. Flunked out the first time he went to West Point and had to reapply for admission. It was his analytical skills that saw him through the second time round." I stood staring at the speaker, my mouth agape. Then I broke into laughter, hooting until tears sprang from my eyes. I felt such relief and joy. And as my laughter subsided, I realized that I was also feeling something else, something that had been missing from my life: hope.

George Patton had struggled with reading and writing as a kid, just like me. But he was gifted with superb analytical skills. I thought about the computer class I had recently taken and loved. I thought about the countless hours I had spent as a child tearing motors apart so I could figure out the functions of the different parts. I had good analytical skills, too! George Patton had made an outstanding success of his life. Maybe I could do well, too.

Spurred on by my new knowledge about Patton, I returned to school, majoring in computer studies. And whenever I found myself in enemy territory, I looked to Patton for inspiration. One of the biggest challenges of my college career came in my senior year, when I took the required English class I'd been putting off for three years. Toward the end of the semester, our professor announced, "For your final exam, which will count for more than half your grade, you will be asked to write a 500-word essay in class, on a topic of your choosing."

My goose is cooked, I told myself. *I'll never be able to do that.* Then I reminded myself of Patton, and his don't-give-up attitude. I sat down and wrote an essay, then asked friends who were good in English to suggest improvements, check my punctuation and correct my myriad spelling errors. Next, I tape-recorded the final product, for I had discovered that it helped me to involve more than one sense when learning difficult material. Listening to the tape while I read the written version, I painstakingly set about memorizing the wording of the essay, the spelling of each word, the placement of each comma, so that I could regurgitate it in class on the day of the exam. It took hours and hours of work—but I passed the course.

That was 15 years ago. Today, many challenges later, I hold an undergraduate degree in Business and Computer Technology, and a masters degree in Business Administration, and I work as a computer consultant. I know that dyslexia will always complicate my existence. But I have made a success of my life. Even better, I have found peace. And all because a man I never met— but have known all my life—gave me the gift of hope.

A resident of Lee's Summit, Missouri, Girard Sagmiller moonlights as a professional model and actor. Through his website (hcity.com/dml.html), he also devotes time to educating the public about dyslexia. His self-published autobiography, Dyslexia My Life, *details how he overcame his disability.*

MIRACULOUS FEET
G. Denise Lance

W hen I was born with cerebral palsy, the doctors told my parents that I would never walk, talk or write my name. But I defied their predictions; in high school I even earned membership in the National Honor Society.

Not that this was an easy accomplishment, for cerebral palsy affects muscle control, and I was unable to write with a pencil or pen. To do written assignments, I devised a way of using a typewriter, but it was a slow and exhausting process. Grasping a stick with both hands, I would press key after key on a typewriter, laboriously forming word after word. My father had made my typing stick from a wooden dowel, fitted with a grip on one end and tapered on the other end, to make it easier for me to hit one key at a time.

About halfway through the first page of a book report or essay, I would experience a familiar agony. My typing could not keep up with my thoughts. As I punched out each word, my mind leaped sentences and paragraphs ahead, and try as I might to hang onto them, some thoughts slipped away like water overflowing a cup already full.

A page or two later, physical fatigue would set in and my arms would become so weak I would have to rest. Not wanting any more thoughts to escape me, I would allow myself to stop for only a moment. But with each additional paragraph, I needed longer breaks. During these periods of inactivity, negative thoughts would creep into my mind, tempting me to quit. *I'm tired. I can't do this any more,* I would tell myself. *The other kids are out having fun, and here I am stuck writing this stupid paper.* Then I would hear another voice, encouraging me to persevere: *You are not those other kids. You'll get a bad grade in English if you don't turn this in. You can't give up. You're almost done.* Dutifully, I would pick up my stick and forge ahead.

Three to five hours after sitting down at the typewriter, I would coach myself through to the end. My inner mantra started with *just one more paragraph*, progressed to *just one more sentence* and then to *just one more word.* To keep up with assignments, I worked seven days a week, eight hours a day. I frequently developed blisters on my hands and cramps in my wrists from holding my typing stick so long. A few times, when I could no longer hold the stick, I typed the last few sentences with my nose.

When I started college, I found the increased workload overwhelming. Typing only eight words per minute, I needed at least seven hours to do a three-page essay. I just couldn't keep up, no matter how many hours I worked, and I dropped out after one semester. I had failed, and for the first time in my 19 years, I felt truly handicapped.

Filled with despair, I began reading inspiring writers such as Norman Vincent Peale. It helped to be reminded that I had been given a unique life that I must live to the fullest despite the obstacles in my path. Finally, after nine months, I found the courage to return to college.

To receive tuition assistance from Vocational Rehabilitation, I had to carry a full course load, but I harbored serious doubts about my ability to handle the work. During my first month back at school, I felt physically sick each morning. My stomach churned, my palms were sweaty and I was barely able to finish breakfast. Nonetheless, I stuck with it and somehow completed two more years, typing with my trusty stick, coaching myself through paper after paper. But by then I was exhausted.

The summer before my junior year, desperate to find a faster means of typing, I asked my father to buy me a computer. "Sure," he agreed. Then, after a moment's hesitation, he asked, "But how are you going to use it?" He was thinking of my attempts to use a computer in high school, which had met with defeat because of my inability to perform certain keystrokes, such as pushing two buttons simultaneously.

"We'll figure that out later," I assured him, although I was not as confident as I tried to sound.

When we brought the computer home, I had an exciting idea. "Put the keyboard on the floor," I told him. "I want to try something." Since my feet were easier to control than my hands, I had always used my toes to dial the telephone and press the buttons on my stereo. Why not try typing with my toes? Scooting my chair up close to the keyboard, which my father had propped at an angle with two phone books, I began pressing keys with my two big toes. The monitor on the table confirmed that I was surprisingly accurate, hitting very few stray keys. And using my toes, I could press two keys at the same time. Dad and I looked at each other. I had found a way to access the computer!

Typing with my toes, I didn't tire as easily. But my typing speed, while improved, was still painfully slow. That same summer, I learned that Tammy, an occupational therapist with whom I had worked, was newly in charge of an Adaptive Computer Technology Program. With mixed feelings of hope and apprehension, I made an appointment with her, knowing that she might be my last hope of easing the task of writing.

During our first meeting, Tammy suggested a technique called scanning. With scanning, the alphabet is displayed on the computer screen, and one by one the letters are highlighted. When the letter I wanted to type was highlighted, I pressed a switch with my foot, and the letter appeared in my document. After just 15 minutes of practice, I was thoroughly discouraged. "This is worse than the way I do things now," I protested, bursting into tears of disappointment.

For several frustrating weeks, Tammy and I tried one thing after another without success. Then one day, she showed me some software that translated abbreviations into words. I could type in the abbreviation "psy," and the word "psychology"—one of my frequently used words—would appear on the computer screen, reducing the number of keys I had to press from ten to three. From the first time I used the program, I knew I had found the answer! Within a few weeks, I was able to type up to 20 words per minute, almost three times as fast as before. I still would not qualify for a clerical position. But then that was never my goal.

With my computer, my abbreviations, and my toes, I finished my undergraduate degree with honors—in just five years. I went on to earn a masters and recently completed my Ph.D. in Special Education. The focus of my graduate studies, and now my work, has been using technology to assist those with disabilities. Who knows, there may be brilliant writers, musicians, scientists, and peacemakers out there, waiting for the right technology to free their talents. And I may be the one to help them discover it.

G. Denise Lance is a technology consultant, web page manager, and freelance writer from Independence, Missouri. She is the creator and manager of the Virtual Assistive Technology Center, a web site offering software for individuals with disabilities.

> *"The best way to eat the elephant standing in your path is to cut it up into little pieces."*
> —African proverb

LETTER TO MY TEACHER

Dear Professor,

I didn't belong in college. I should have told you that. My father dropped out of school after third grade. My mother went through twelfth grade, but her family thought she was a little uppity for doing so. Like my mother, I finished high school, and immediately got married and started having babies. A decade and a half later, I was a divorced single parent, working as a babysitter during the day and clerking part-time nights in a food store. My income fell far below the poverty level, where, I'd lived for much of my life. Statisticians said I didn't belong in college. Who was I to argue?

But one night when I was emptying the trash at the end of my shift, I noticed a brightly colored catalog in the dumpster behind the store. I fished it out and wiped the ketchup drips off the cover. Flipping through the catalog later, I discovered it listed all the courses available at the local college.

And I discovered something else: Taking only one course would make me eligible for student health insurance. Neither of my jobs included benefits, and every time my kids came down with a cold, I worried about what would happen to us if we were really sick. I did some careful calculations. If I took one college course each semester for a year, the cost of tuition, books and fees would be far lower than even six months of private insurance. My two kids would be covered, too. What a deal!

Becoming a student was a great scheme. But I knew, when I took my first course from you, that I was an impostor.

The very first day of that sociology class, you made an announcement that threatened to expose me. "At the end of the semester, each student will be required to make an oral presentation," you told us.

My stomach began to churn relentlessly at the thought of speaking in front of the class. "How was school today, honey?" my youngest daughter greeted me when I got home, doing a creditable imitation of my usual after-school question to her. But I was already halfway down the hall to the bathroom where I promptly lost my lunch.

Weeks passed before I could sit through class without nausea. I talked myself into going to class each day by telling myself, over and over, that I was doing this for my kids. I went early to claim the only safe seat—back row, aisle. Close to the door. Just in case. Back with the whisperers and the snoozers, behind the tall man who always read the student newspaper during class, I chewed the fingernails on one hand while I took notes with the other.

I needed three credits. I didn't need the agony of a presentation. I considered dropping your course and signing up for something else. Anything else. But I stayed, although I didn't know why. You were new to teaching, and your lectures certainly weren't polished. You gripped the lectern like a shield and sometimes your voice died out in the middle of a sentence. But your enthusiasm for your subject left me longing to know more. I looked forward to a few quiet hours each week—those rare times when the store was empty or my little ones were napping—that I spent reading, writing, and thinking about what I'd heard in your class.

One day while I was thinking, I recalled a fascinating lecture you had given on the importance of defining terms. And I noticed that your syllabus hadn't defined "oral presentation." Perhaps I had discovered a way out of the ordeal I dreaded. When the time came for my presentation at the end of the semester, I carried a tape recorder to the front of the room, pushed "play," and returned to my seat, where I listened with the other students to the oral presentation I'd taped the night before.

When I signed up for the next course you taught, a course on women who had shaped American culture and history, I expected you would require another oral presentation. But I figured a little agony while I started a tape recorder wouldn't be so bad.

In this second course, you came out from behind the lectern and moved up and down the aisles as you spoke. You often stood at the back of the room when you made an important point. Whispering and sleeping ceased when you did that; all heads turned in your direction. You spoke confidently and smoothly, and you called on us by name.

I was so caught up in the class that a few weeks passed before I read the syllabus carefully. Then I found your long and precise definition of "oral presentation," a definition that excluded the use of tape recorders. To be sure I understood, you stopped by my desk one day and said, "This time, I want it *live!*"

College was sharpening my critical thinking skills, and I put those skills to work when choosing the subject for my presentation. I would speak about Lucretia Mott, a Quaker feminist. When my turn dawned, I came to class dressed like Lucretia, in a long skirt and shawl, a black bonnet covering most of my face. Standing before the other students, I spoke in the first person. Acting a part, I felt as if someone else were giving that presentation.

***

By the time we met again in the classroom, I had had to admit to myself that I was in college for more than my health. I'd scraped together enough credits to be one quarter away from graduation. I had a lean program of study that allowed no frills, just the courses essential for my degree. Your course didn't fit my program, but I decided to take it anyway, and I skipped lunch for weeks to pay for the extra credits.

When you handed back our first exam, mine had a note scribbled alongside the grade. You said you wanted me to give my presentation for this course. Not a tape recorder. Not a persona. My body tensed and my breathing grew shallow as I felt the same panic that had gripped me during my first course with you. My only comfort came from knowing that by the time I recovered from fainting during my presentation, the quarter would be over and I would have my degree.

You didn't lecture in this course. You pushed the lectern into

> *"I think I can."*   —The Little Engine That Could

a corner and arranged our chairs in a circle. You sat with us, your voice one among many. You gave direction to discussions that we carried on long after class periods officially ended. I came early, not to claim an escape seat but to share ideas with other students. I stayed late to be part of the continuing conversation.

Three can be a magic number. One day, toward the end of that third course, you turned to me and said, "Kate, would you share with the class what you've learned about the dangers of moving elderly folks from one living place to another?" This was the subject I'd been researching for my presentation, and I knew it cold. I rose and moved to the chalkboard to draw a graph of my findings. Then I stood in front of the class, speaking in my own voice, just as I had spoken during our discussion circles. I was five minutes into my talk when it hit me: I was giving a presentation. My heartbeat accelerated, but I kept my attention on the interested faces before me, and the moment of panic passed. I remember thinking, as I walked back to my seat, that I wasn't an impostor in the classroom any more. I belonged in that room as much as anyone.

I was happy when you stopped to speak with me after class. I thought you might congratulate me on surviving the presentation or on finishing the coursework for my bachelor's degree. Instead, you asked where I planned to go to graduate school.

You were doing it again! Every time I crept over the line between the familiar and the unknown, you pushed the line a little farther forward. I steamed out of the classroom. *She has already forced me to talk in front of people*, I thought resentfully —or at least, partly so. *I'm getting the first college degree in my family. And now she wants more?*

Weeks later—after graduation, after I'd read all the mindless magazines on the rack at work, after I'd thought about life without the stimulation of classes—I cooled down. And applied to graduate school.

I wonder if you knew that the only way I could finance my graduate degree would be by teaching classes as a graduate assistant, a challenge that initially cost me many a sleepless night. The first time my voice gave out in the middle of a lecture, I remembered you. I realized then that you had felt as nervous while teaching as I had felt being taught. I looked over the lectern at a room full of people, many of whom probably felt as I once had: nervous, unsure, but anxious to learn. And I stopped the lecture and arranged the chairs in a circle.

So I write this letter to say thanks. Thanks for opening the circle and thanks for opening my mind. And thanks for giving me a push when I needed it.

By the way, my graduate degree opened up a great job for me. Yes, you guessed it—I'm teaching at a university. With health insurance.

Gratefully,

Kate Boyes

Kate Boyes, who writes by the light of candles and kerosene lamps because she chooses to live without electricity, is the author of a monthly magazine column on living simply, as well as poems and essays. A resident of Smithfield, Utah, she is also a writer-in-residence in public schools.

SECTION VII

♦TRIALS OF WORKING HOURS♦

"Don't worry about genius. Don't worry about being clever. Trust to hard work, perseverance and determination. And the best motto for a long march is: Don't grumble. Plug on!"
—SIR THOMAS TREVES

RATTLING JAIL DOORS
Tekla Dennison Miller

When my telephone rang at 3:30 that Friday afternoon in April, most employees had already fled north for a weekend at lake cottages. I took a deep, tired breath as I lifted the receiver and answered, "Warden Miller."

"This is Joyce Cambridge. Sorry to bother you so late in the day, but we've got a problem at the men's prison." Ms. Cambridge was a lawyer for the Michigan Department of Corrections, and I was in charge of the Huron Valley Women's Prison—not the men's prison next door.

"I'm not sure why you're calling me," I replied.

"I'm just going by this memo from Deputy Director Burke. It clearly states that, as of today, you are the warden of the men's prison."

This was my first hint that I had a new job but I received confirmation a few minutes later, when the deputy director called. My shoulders slumped at Burke's announcement: "Sorry I couldn't get there today to tell you this in person but an emergency came up. Due to budget cuts, you'll be running the men's prison along with the women's prison, effective immediately."

Hanging up the phone, I began to digest Burke's news. I was now warden of two maximum security prisons and 1,100 inmates, with the majority of the men locked down 23 hours a day. I turned to the wall behind my desk. Next to the state seal hung a picture of a pig with wings flying over the rainbow. Its caption read, "Soar above the ordinary." I smiled even as I contemplated the mammoth task ahead of me.

The following Monday, I pulled my car into the spot reserved for the warden of the men's prison. I hadn't slept well over the weekend. I would be facing a staff that was almost entirely male and known for not welcoming women coworkers.

As I entered the lobby, Deputy Warden Mayer, my new second-in-command, rushed up and blocked my passage. His eyes were hidden behind the dark glasses he always wore, which added to his menacing appearance. "I'm not going to mince any words with you," he declared, in a voice loud enough for the lobby officer to hear. "A woman should not run a men's max."

His boldness startled me but I was careful not to show any emotion as I shrugged, "I guess we're both going to have to get used to it." I sighed with relief when he stomped off.

Are you prepared for this? I asked myself. I wanted to bolt. Instead, I told myself: *You've never run from a tough situation before and you're not going to do that now.*

I half smiled at the officer who let me through the locked gates onto the grounds of the prison. Though he acknowledged me with an efficient nod, his eyes glimmered with disdain. I could feel his hostile stare burning into my back as I set out on my rounds.

"Nice legs." "You sure smell good!" The prisoners' impetuous greetings were inappropriate, but I let it go, for at least they seemed pleased to see me, unlike my staff. Then, leaving Unit Three, I heard one prisoner yell out to a woman officer, "Hey tramp, get me a light." She did as he commanded. I looked to the unit's sergeant for a reaction. He didn't lift his head from the count sheets he was reviewing.

"Sergeant Bates!" I shouted over the ever-present din of prisoner voices.

He raised his head. "Ma'am?"

"Is it normal for prisoners to address a woman officer as 'tramp'?"

His face reddened but he did not respond.

The cellblock became so quiet you could hear the prisoners

breathing. In a commanding voice, I announced, "From now on, Sergeant, you'll write up any prisoner for making degrading comments to officers, especially women. And I will not speak to any prisoner who is loud or disrespectful."

Sergeant Bates' mouth tightened. I asked, "Do you understand?"

He didn't back away. "Yes ma'am."

"Good."

I walked to the door of the prisoner who had called the officer "tramp." "Move this man to an inside cell," I told the officer whom he had insulted.

"Man. I can't see nothin' from the inside," the prisoner whined.

"Right. And that's what will happen to any prisoner that mouths off." I stared into his eyes. When he leaned away from the cell door window, I left. My heels clicked like hail hitting a metal roof as I strode out of the silent block.

A few days later, while making rounds, I watched as a belligerent prisoner was sprayed with pepper gas. Once subdued, he was extracted from his cell by a five-man team, dubbed a "goon squad" by the inmates. I observed that male officers from the unit and from other areas of the prison made up the team, while women officers on the unit stood by.

Immediately, I called Deputy Mayer to my office. He entered without knocking and slid into a chair opposite my desk, his smile cool and arrogant.

"Who gave the orders to gas that prisoner?"

"I did," he replied, as he raised his hands, palms up.

"You're not authorized to do that. From now on such orders will come from me. And starting now, you will have women on the extraction teams."

Mayer stood up, placed both hands on my desk and leaned toward me: "That's a crazy idea. They can't handle it."

"Try them." I said, bending forward, eye to eye with him. "What kind of signal do you think you're giving prisoners about women?"

He didn't answer.

"Let me clue you in," I said. "You're telling them women are weak and can't do an officer's job. You're setting them up to get harassed and possibly injured."

After a few moments, Mayer turned and started for the door. He stopped suddenly and faced me. "My officers won't like this."

I grinned. "Maybe some of the men won't, but they'll get used to it."

His lip curled as he snarled, "I'll never get used to it."

That night, I got the first of many threatening phone calls. The next day, the prison mail brought me the first of a weekly series of anonymous typewritten threats. But none of these was as frightening as the scare I received three months later, when a psychiatrist phoned to warn me, "The officer you recently fired has threatened to kill you, and I believe he will try to do it."

As I hung up, my heart was beating so hard I could see my chest move with its rhythm. Finally I called the shift commander, my hand tight around the receiver, beads of sweat above my lips. "Put an armed guard on the front door," I ordered. "And alert every gun tower officer." I hoped none of those armed officers held a grudge against me.

Two nights later, I was forced onto the shoulder of the highway by a speeding truck. I never knew whether it was an accident or the action of a disgruntled employee, but I never stopped looking in the rearview mirror after that. Nightmares about stalkers intruded on my sleep, and I was afraid to open any door to an unexpected knock.

Fortunately, by the end of a long, tough year, the personal threats against me had dwindled, and many staffers at the men's prison had come over to my side. They even contributed ideas for constructive programming and incentives for inmates. But behind my back, some officers still called me Leona of the Valleys, after Leona Helmsley, known as "The Queen of Mean." I realized that several male employees remained intimidated by change.

That point was brought home at a memorable officers' union meeting. I listened attentively as the all-male leadership complained bitterly, "It's just not like it used to be. You've changed everything."

Responding, I kept my tone neutral. "All I'm asking is that you follow policy."

The union president shook his head in disgust. "Yeah, that's what they told us you'd say: follow policy."

"Are there far fewer assaults?"

He hesitated, then nodded his head. "Yeah."

I raised my eyebrows and lifted my hands as though I were offering him a gift. "Are there far fewer injuries?"

"Yeah."

"Do you think the changes might be working?"

He leaned back and looked at the others in the room and then at me. "Yeah. . . But it's not the same."

"Yeah," I said with a big smile.

Tekla Dennison Miller, author of The Warden Wore Pink *(Biddle Publishing), is the former warden of two maximum security prisons outside Detroit, Michigan. She is a now a criminal justice consultant in Colorado.*

TASTE OF VICTORY
Rachel Peña Roos

*T*ranquilo. There'll be room for all 32 of you on this 15-passenger bus. *Tranquilo.* Another three months, and you'll be speaking Spanish like a native. *Tranquilo.* This isn't even close to how hot it gets here.

Tranquilo: Be patient. Relax. Take it easy.

I'd come to Paraguay as a Peace Corps volunteer and I had big plans. I had goals. I had an agenda. I had very specifically defined how I would measure my success. I had trouble being *tranquilo.*

Perhaps it was because of growing up in America, perhaps it was just me, but patience was a virtue I'd always had trouble understanding. And now I was more confused than ever. I thought we were in Paraguay to help. I thought we were there to make a difference. I didn't think we were there to relax.

And yet, during my three months of training, every time I turned around, I heard that word: *Tranquilo. Tranquilo. Tranquilo.* I heard it from trainers, from bus drivers, from my host family. In cafes, in the market, in the health center. And always it was delivered with a calm, friendly smile.

At the end of the training, I couldn't wait to get to the village where I would live and work. At last I could begin doing all the things I had told myself I would accomplish.

I was based in Kera'y, a rural village of 500, set in the lush, gently rolling hills of south central Paraguay. My assignment involved a variety of basic but important tasks. I visited schools to teach children about the importance of eating healthy foods and brushing their teeth. I worked with a Paraguayan nurse to organize and run PAP campaigns and educate women about the dangers of cervical cancer. I started a community garden with some teachers and their students. I helped Paraguayans and other Peace Corps volunteers build sanitary latrines. I worked with the community to help establish a health clinic.

I was doing stuff. But I couldn't help but feel I could be doing more—if it wasn't for *tranquilo.*

Tranquilo. The supplies will get here.

Tranquilo. The pigs don't know they're supposed to stay out of the garden.

Tranquilo. It gets much hotter than this.

The work I was most proud of, and the best times I spent in Paraguay, involved the Mothers Club, which I helped establish soon after I reached my village. We met once a week at a mother's house or at the river to do laundry and bathe. While we worked, we talked and learned from one another. These women soon became my family. They warmly welcomed me into their homes, where they treated me as a daughter, a sister, a granddaughter or a good friend.

I always had an agenda for our club meetings. A topic for discussion. A list of things I wanted to accomplish. We would talk about ways to improve nutrition and their diets, breast-feeding, pregnancy, vaccinations, first aid—just about anything that was related to keeping moms and their kids healthy.

But my goal was to do more than simply talk with the women. I wanted to see results. I wanted my community to have the lowest rate of cervical cancer in all of Paraguay. I wanted the Ministry of Health to single out my village as the only community in the country with absolutely no intestinal parasites. I wanted every family to eat a nutritious diet. And I wanted all of this now.

Tranquilo. Things cannot change overnight.

Tranquilo. More people will show up for your next workshop.

Tranquilo. We can talk about that later. Let's have some tea first.

One of my pet projects was an effort to get villagers to include broccoli in their diets. It grew like crazy in the fields surrounding the village but none of the mothers knew how to prepare it. Every week I would remind my friends in the Mothers Club about the many wonderful qualities of broccoli: its availability, its nutritional value, its ease of preparation. Yet in this area, as in so many others, I felt I was getting nowhere.

One day, about a year into my service, I was waiting in front of my neighbor's house for a bus to the Paraguayan capital, Asunción. It had rained a few days earlier and the roads were muddy. It looked as though the bus might never arrive. I paced back and forth and mumbled to myself. *Tranquilo.* I told myself, the bus will be here soon. I paced some more. *Tranquilo,* the bus will be here soon. Frustrated, I sat down heavily on the ground.

A while later, I looked up to see little Maria, the daughter of one of the women in my Mothers Club. "*Tranquilo,*" she said. "The bus will be here soon."

I managed a slight smile and noticed that she was holding a plate of tortillas that her mother had sent. She sat down next to me and handed me one. I bit into it—and let go of my time line. Suddenly the heat and the pigs in the garden seemed bearable. Maria Brizuela's mother had put broccoli in her tortillas!

And not just for me. Maria said that her mother was cooking broccoli in lots of different foods. She said that her father was even learning to like it.

Maria left, and I stayed waiting for the bus. *Tranquilo,* I said to myself. It doesn't matter when the bus comes. For the family of Juan de Dios eats broccoli.

Rachel Peña Roos lives in Nevada City, California, and is a social worker for the Nevada County Children's Protective Service.

RIDE ON, BOBBY!

"Wanted. Young, skinny, wiry fellows. Must be expert riders. Willing to risk death daily. Orphans preferred."

—1860 newspaper ad for Pony Express riders

Robert Haslam, known as "Pony Bob," was given the most important assignment of his career as a rider for the Pony Express in February, 1861. Newly elected president Abraham Lincoln was about to take office, and the Pony Express had been asked to deliver a telegraphed transcript of his inaugural speech from Missouri to California. The nation was on the verge of civil war, and California lawmakers were debating which side to take. Lincoln's speech might influence the decision substantially—if it were received in time—and the Pony Express wanted to assure the speediest delivery possible. Pony Bob was handpicked to be part of the relay team that would get the job done.

He was chosen to ride a 120-mile stretch in western Nevada inhabited by hostile Paiutes. During a two-month rampage the previous year, tribal members had destroyed seven Pony Express relay stations, killing 15 employees.

Pony Bob was expecting an ambush and, sure enough, early in his ride, he found himself surrounded by mounted warriors, some on stolen Pony Express horses. He outran the Indian ponies, but knew he could not outdistance the six stolen horses, which, after all, had been chosen by the Pony Express for their speed. Regretfully, Bob pulled out one of his two six-shooters and began killing these fine steeds. Three horses remained alive, and the Indians riding them fought back; one letting fly an arrow that pierced Haslam's left arm, hitting the bone. Pony Bob spurred his horse faster. He turned and fired three shots at the head of the horse right behind him. It fell to the ground, and the second horse plowed into it, losing its

footing. The one Pauite still in pursuit drew his bow. An arrow tore through Bob's lip, breaking his jaw and knocking out five teeth. Struggling to remain conscious, the Pony Express rider fired his remaining bullets into the chest of the last horse.

When he reached the next relay station, Pony Bob stuffed a clean rag in his mouth to check the flow of blood, mounted a fresh horse, and kept on riding. Eight hours after setting out, he reached his destination and handed off Lincoln's speech to a new rider.

When Lincoln's speech finally arrived in Sacramento, Pony Bob and his fellow riders had completed the trip between St. Joseph, Missouri and Sacramento in a record seven days and 17 hours, shaving over two days from the Pony Express's usual delivery time. California stuck with the Union, and Pony Bob, incidentally, lived to the ripe old age of 72.

STEEL NERVES: WALKING THE WALK
Merril Mushroom

W|hen I was in my 20s and 30s, I lived in a big city, where I made my living as a schoolteacher. Shortly before my 40th birthday, I moved to a small rural town in the hills of Tennessee. But I was unable to find a teaching position there so I began looking around for other jobs.

A nuclear power plant was being built in the area. Because the project was federally funded, the construction company in charge was obliged to hire minorities. Both "older" and a woman, I qualified on two counts. Deep in my heart, I did not consider myself a prime candidate for a construction crew: I was not adventurous, nor was I physically skilled. Although I was tall and big-boned, I was slow-moving and clumsy. But I was desperate for work so I applied for a carpenter's apprenticeship, and was hired.

My first day on the job, I was overwhelmed by the sheer size of the construction project, the mammoth machinery, the ear-splitting noise. Tower cranes swung huge stacks of lumber overhead and concrete trucks rumbled to and fro with loads to pour. I soon realized that I was the only woman among hundreds of men, all of whom believed that a woman had her place, and that it was definitely not on their construction site, an attitude most of them expressed by ignoring me totally.

The work itself was exhausting. I was assigned to a crew putting up 15-foot-high walls for concrete pours on a wide expanse of flooring. After the first hour of hammering nails, my arm felt as if it would fall off, but I pushed myself to keep going. That afternoon, I locked myself in a smelly porta-john to cry in secret.

I was grateful, however, to be working on solid ground, grateful that I didn't have to climb the swaying rebar steel walls or, worse yet, work above the deep pit dubbed "The Hole." This pit, the size of a football field, was canopied by a grid of rebar an inch in diameter, criss-crossed at right angles. Sometimes I would see men working out there, balanced on the steel, and the very sight caused my stomach to clutch. The bars provided unstable footing and were spaced far enough apart that anyone who stumbled might slip through and fall, to be shattered on the concrete surface eight feet below. How anyone could venture onto this grid was beyond my comprehension.

A couple months after I began work, I arrived at the construction site to find the carpenter's helper waiting for me. "Come on," he said. "You're being changed to Ray's crew." Then he added, "Ray don't like women on construction." And off he set, without looking back.

As I followed him, I remembered that apprentices changed crews every two months. *Ray doesn't like women on construction, huh?* I thought. Then the helper stopped, and all thoughts of Ray fled from my mind. "Oh no," I moaned. We stood before The Hole, and the helper was talking to a burly foreman and pointing at me. The foreman glanced at me and frowned, turned his back, walked to the edge of a nearby cliff, stepped down and descended out of sight.

I barely heard the helper's farewell. I stared about desperately, my thoughts racing wildly. *This must be a mistake. The helper must have brought me here by accident. No, don't even think about accidents!*

I walked to the edge of the cliff and looked over. The men in the crew were on a ledge about 30 feet down. A rickety wood ladder rested against the rock face of the cliff. I swallowed hard. I'd promised myself never to lay foot on one of those ill-constructed structures, which the carpenters on the crew built to use as needed. Now it seemed I'd have to break that promise, but my terror prevented me from slinging my leg over the cliff and stepping onto the ladder. *Go on then,* I rebuked myself silently. *You may as well turn around and go home. Then the men can say they were right all along—that women don't belong in construction. And you'll be out of a job, with no way to support your kids.* I swallowed again and looked over the cliff. The top rung of the ladder was two feet below the edge, and there was nothing to hold on to.

I have to do this! I thought. I turned my back to the edge of the cliff, got down on all fours, and reached down with my right foot until it met the second rung of the ladder. Holding my breath, I rested the top of my body against the cliff wall, eased my other foot down to the third rung, stepped with all my weight, and grabbed the top rung with clammy hands. *Whew! That was every bit as bad as I thought it would be.* Shifting sideways to free the pouches of my tool belt, which had caught on the rungs, I took a deep breath and tried to calm my pounding heart. Then the whistle blew, signaling the start of the work shift.

I reached the bottom of the ladder in time to see the men swarming over the edge of yet another cliff and down a shorter ladder—and suddenly I felt faint. I had forgotten my ultimate, terrifying destination.

I stared out over that ocean of thin-lined squares with empty middles. The men ahead of me struggled across, teetering precariously from side to side. My self-congratulations over descending the ladder evaporated into despair.

By the time I got down the second ladder, an electrician on the edge of The Hole was playing out a lead for the welder, while at the center of the web of rebar, journeymen were plugging in saws and drills, stacking lumber, and setting down boards upon which to place sawhorses. My stomach tightened, squeezing my breakfast until I could feel every bite. I couldn't imagine getting out there, never mind working there. *I give up*, I told myself. *I can't do this.*

"Better come on." I looked up to see the electrician heading out over the steel. "They ain't much for working with a woman on this crew, and they won't like you shirkin'."

I really can't do this. A knot choked my throat. *I'm too afraid. What if I fall? I can't!*

But I knew I had to. Tentatively, I took one step onto the steel. The bar moved beneath my boot, and I was hit by such a surge of fear that I almost passed out. I shifted my foot slightly and stepped out until my arch rested where the bars crossed. Then I looked out over The Hole. About midway to where the men worked, a ring of vertical steel rose from the floor grid. If I could get to that, maybe I could hold on while I made my way closer to where the guys were. Farther on, I noticed a piece of plywood lying flat on the steel, an island of safety. Maybe I could move

> *"If I were asked to give what I consider the single most useful bit of advice for all humanity it would be this: Expect trouble as an inevitable part of life and when it comes, hold your head high, look it squarely in the eye and say, I will be bigger than you. You cannot defeat me."*
>
> —Ann Landers

over from the vertical steel to stand on it.

I raised my left foot from the secure rock ledge and brought it up even with the foot already poised on the rebar. Now I was committed, for I could not back up, and I could not turn around. Shifting my feet, one after the other, onto raised intersections of rebar, I progressed from one square to another, fixing my eyes on the vertical steel as it came closer and closer, until I could grab the bars. Hand over hand, I made my way toward the plywood, until finally, I was standing on it. I took a few moments to catch my breath, and then I joined the crew.

I walked steel in trepidation for many weeks. But if I did not conquer my fear, neither did it conquer me. And over time, it ebbed away, until finally I was able to walk steel with ease and confidence.

Merril Mushroom's work has been published in women's anthologies and periodicals.

THE FUTURE WAS MINE TO SEE
Sylvia Halliday

Did you fall down? Pick yourself up."

That's what my mother used to say when I was small and tripped over my feet. Not "Poor little thing." Just "Pick yourself up."

It was said with warmth and sympathy, but at the same time the lesson was clear: Bad things sometimes happen. Get on with your life.

Still, the lesson was hard to remember when, after 42 years, four kids, and two grandkids, my marriage came to an end. Or, more precisely, I threw out my husband.

As you might expect, there was another woman. She was his business partner as well as his mistress, and their pie-in-the-sky schemes had drained our finances. I had been a moderately successful novelist for some time when I discovered that I'd been supporting us so that he could support her, and their dreams of instant wealth. It became clear to me that she had his love, his loyalty, what money he had, and his nine-to-five attention. In short, everything but his dirty socks. So I let her have *them*.

The next nine months were sheer hell. I was emotionally devastated and, financially, I was in a real pickle, left with a Manhattan co-op I couldn't afford. My husband, who had a pile of unpaid bills, was no help. To add to my woes, I found I had major writer's block. Dozens of plots danced in my head, but I'd neither the will nor the ability to commit them to paper. My keyboard gathered dust.

The future looked bleak. No money, no husband, stalled career. I was over the hill but not quite old enough to collect Social Security. I put the co-op on the market, preparing to scale down my lifestyle drastically. But meanwhile, I had to eat.

What the hell could I do? I'd never held a real job. As was typical of women in my generation, I'd gone from college to marriage to motherhood. The writing had been a middle-aged fluke, astonishing me with its success. I felt worthless, incompetent, panicky. And old.

Then a writing friend told me that he could get me a job, doing what he did to tide himself over the rough spots.

"Anything!" I said.

"It's kind of embarrassing," he said, hesitating a bit.

I was desperate. "If it's legal and I'm able, I'll do it," I insisted. "But what is it?"

"I'm a telephone psychic," he said.

Telephone psychic? He might as well have said he was a rodeo show groupie!

But he persisted. "It pays $11 an hour and you can work as many hours as you want, day or night. The callers see the TV ads for free psychic readings and dial the main office. If you're logged on, they route the calls to you and you're in business. You use a phony name, and no one knows your number." He obtained a contract for me to sign. Then he loaned me a deck of Tarot cards, gave me a couple of books on card readings, and ran me through a few practice sessions, assuring me I could do it.

I took a couple of days to work up my courage. Then, one night at midnight, "Victoria" logged on. I pulled out a handful of cards that represented areas of concern I might be dealing with, having decided to use the same seven cards for every call.

The phone rang almost at once. "You're speaking to Victoria," I said in my most all-seeing, all-knowing tone. "May I have your full name and address, and your age, please?" (The name and address would be saved for the end of the call, when I'd try to pitch the caller a subscription to some psychic magazine; determining age was a legal necessity since, after ten free minutes, every minute cost $4.95!)

My first caller was Susie from North Carolina. I listened carefully to her every inflection, hoping to get a clue to her frame of mind. As a mother, I had developed the skill early on of listening for the lie, the evasion, the hidden troubles.

"I'm going to use the Tarot cards to help solve your problems," I said. "Can you hear me shuffling the deck?" This was always the trickiest part: I'd riffle part of the deck near the phone, with the instrument hooked under my ear. But since I was also holding a pencil to make notes, as well as the ever-present cigarette to keep me calm, I could have used as many arms as Kali, the Hindu goddess!

Knowing I was expected to keep the caller on the phone more than ten minutes, I slowly described the cards I was supposedly dealing out: the three of Cups, the Tower, the Moon, the five of Swords, and so on. Eventually, I "divined" that Susie was mourning her mother's passing. "The cards tell me your mother is smiling down from Heaven," I told her comfortingly, adding a heavy dose of genuine sympathy and encouragement to forge ahead. I even managed to sell her a subscription.

The phone rang again as soon as I hung up. Joe from West Virginia. With a desperate edge in his young voice.

"Cups refer to love," I said. "So there seems to be some problem there. And Pentacles mean money worries. Especially since I dealt out the eight of Pentacles. That tells me you're experiencing financial difficulties." (An easy guess. What young person isn't?)

"You're amazing!" he exclaimed. "It's my ex-wife."

"Of course," I said confidently. "The cards tell me there are problems with alimony."

He whistled in amazement. "Yeah! She keeps bugging me!"

I silently cursed all deadbeat ex-husbands, but kept my voice calm and filled with understanding. "The presence of the Tower card indicates that you are a rock of strength. Someone your ex-wife looks up to. If you fulfill your obligations to her, you can look forward to a stable and solid future."

"But what am I supposed to do about my girlfriend?" he whined. "She wants to go to Disneyland. That costs a bundle. And if I don't make a car payment soon, I'll lose the darn thing."

"Yes, the cards tell me your plate is full," I said dryly. Suggesting he take care of old problems before taking on new ones, I restrained the impulse to yell, "You have money problems? Then why the hell are you spending $4.95 a minute on this?"

I logged off at six a.m., exhilarated. I had made it through the night. The phone had never stopped ringing and, although lots of callers had simply hung up at the end of ten minutes, I had turned a profit for the company.

My best caller had been a Rutgers student who didn't understand why he couldn't attract more girls. After running through the litany of the cards and getting nowhere, I threw in the towel.

"Look," I said. "Do you want to hear what the cards say, or would you prefer the advice of a mother of three grown sons?"

"Oh, wow!" he said. "Mothers know best. What am I doing wrong?"

He was good for 35 minutes. I hope he got the girl.

I worked at the job for nearly two months and made grocery money, at least. But I had to keep reminding myself that I was supposed to be psychic. "It seems to me . . ." I'd begin, then quickly correct myself, "That is, the cards tell me . . ." And I simply couldn't stretch out many calls beyond the first ten minutes. I preferred quick, helpful advice to endless, mystical bull.

My friend tried to help me. I told him about the caller who had asked for help in finding his lost keys, and confessed that I'd responded by saying, "If I was that good a psychic, I wouldn't be doing this!"

"I would have found the keys," my friend replied, coaching me. "You can do ten minutes alone on seeing water in the cards—a sink, a lake, a river. They may spend the next two days hunting for the damn keys in every liquid they can think of, but at least you've kept them on the phone!"

However, I was far too practical, honest and analytical to really dish the line. And there is a basic incompatibility between being a "psychic" and a Jewish Mother, genuinely eager to help people. I was a low earner, and the company routed fewer and fewer calls to me. We eventually dissolved the contract by mutual consent.

But I had discovered, much to my joy and surprise, that I knew how to pick myself up. That no legitimate job was beneath me. That merely living had given me untapped skills. And that I could do whatever I had to.

I could survive.

Sylvia Halliday has written 14 historical romances. She lives in Queens, New York.

THE TIRE WASN'T BUILT IN A DAY

Charles Goodyear had already obtained patents on an improved water faucet and an air pump when, in 1834, rubber caught his attention. Rubber products, made of the sap of a Brazilian tree, had become an American fad. But rubber companies were going broke and the industry seemed doomed because of the substance's unfortunate habit of changing with the temperature. Raincoats and life preservers that were serviceable in the spring became hard and brittle in the winter. With the onset of summer heat, they took on the qualities of masticated, very smelly chewing gum.

Goodyear turned the kitchen in his Philadelphia home into a laboratory for his experiments, cooking rubber, mixing it with other substances, and treating its surface with various chemicals. He took his mission into debtors' prison where, behind bars, he kept on mixing and testing. Once released, he redoubled his efforts, slowed only by lack of cash and chronic stomach problems that forced him to bed for days and weeks.

The engaging Goodyear enlisted the support of one backer after another, but between backers, he and his family lived in poverty. More than once, his rubber obsession reduced him to auctioning off the household furnishings. After the dishes had been sold, he crafted plates and bowls of rubber for the family's use. By the late 1830s, most of his friends viewed him as a bit of a nut case. But Goodyear, like the material he was working on, kept bouncing back.

Goodyear had moved to the Boston area, and it was there, in January 1839, that he accidentally dropped a piece of rubber compounded with sulfur on a hot wood stove. He removed the rubber from the stove and examined it carefully. What he saw thrilled him. Instead of melting as rubber usually did when exposed to heat, it charred like leather and was firm and flexible. Left out in the cold overnight, it retained these qualities. The answer to his quest was a combination of sulfur and very high heat!

There were further setbacks over the next few years, including two more stays in debtors' prison, as Goodyear set about perfecting the process he had discovered. At one low point, suffering from a painful attack of gout, he hobbled eight miles to Boston through drifts of snow, hoping to secure a loan from an acquaintance, only to meet with failure. The following day he limped home to find his two-year-old sick and dying.

Goodyear persisted, believing he was an instrument of Providence. Finally, in 1844, he obtained a patent on his process, which came to be called vulcanization—and which later made possible the production of automobile tires. Manufacturers began to purchase licenses to employ Goodyear's process. The inventor never made much money, while others built a fortune on his discovery. However, he was deeply satisfied at having accomplished his goal. "Life should not be estimated exclusively by the standard of dollars and cents . . ." he wrote in his autobiography. "A man has cause for regret only when he sows and no one reaps."

MILITARY MOM
Tracy Price Thompson

I t was well before sunrise on Christmas morning, the time of day those of us serving in the military call "O-dark-thirty." The city of Newport News, Va., lay still and cold under a blanket of sleet and snow. I struggled out of bed and began to get ready for work, my heart devoid of holiday spirit. I was the single mother of three —my older son was nearly eight, a second son had just turned four, and my baby girl was not quite three—yet the Army had not an ounce of sympathy for my exacting family situation. *Why do I have to work on Christmas?* I lamented inwardly.

The worst part was I had to leave my children alone. I was newly divorced and we had only recently taken up residence at Fort Eustis. As usual, we were hundreds of miles from others in my family, and I had yet to forge any close friendships on the base. The childcare center was closed, of course, and I'd searched high and low for a babysitter, without success. Never mind that I couldn't afford to pay a babysitter, even if I'd found one, what with my every dollar budgeted down to the penny. Christmas is for families, and yet I had no one I could ask to take in my little ones on this day.

Quietly, I slipped into my government-issue long johns, battle fatigues and thick woolen socks. I gathered my camouflage hat, cold-weather gloves and heavy combat boots, and reluctantly descended the stairs. The lights on our Christmas tree blinked a multicolored "good morning" in my direction, and I jerked their plugs from the electrical sockets, extinguishing the false cheer that could not penetrate my aching heart. Outside in the icy darkness, I told myself that this was by far the worst Christmas of my life.

"Baby, you're an excellent mommy," my mother had often told me. "No matter what comes your way, you manage to handle things without complaining or losing your cool." But as I drove to work, I was all out of answers, and my back felt bruised from being pushed against one wall after another.

I'd only recently been reunited with the children after a year-long tour in Saudi Arabia. There had been many nights that I'd stood at the railing of the barge that served as my home, longing to hold my children. After my return to the States, I'd been anxious to gather the four of us under one roof and resume a semblance of normal family life, and I'd been ecstatic to land government quarters immediately after signing onto the base. But here I was, and here we were, apart on Christmas morn.

What made this even more difficult was the knowledge that I would soon be separated from the kids again. I was working as an aircraft-load planner for the troops and cargo departing daily for Somalia, West Africa. In just three weeks, when the last aircraft was loaded and airborne, my name would be added to the passenger manifest. I would be the last soldier deployed to Somalia. My parents had offered to care for my children in my absence. I was very grateful for that, but my coming departure loomed gloomily this day.

I reported to work at Langley Air Force Base, some 30 minutes from Fort Eustis, at 4:45 A.M., but mentally I was still at home. Leaving the children unsupervised was not only against my motherly instincts, it was also strictly against military regulations.

I reviewed my efforts to ensure the kids' safety. The previous night I'd given my firstborn, Kharim, explicit instructions as to what he should do. "All of the toys are set out and put together except the electric train set," I'd told him. "Don't try to use it; I'll assemble it when I get home." I also reminded him, "Do not answer the telephone unless you are sure it's me on the line. You

---

FORTITUDE IN BLACK AND WHITE

"Mac had guts when it took guts to have guts." Those were the elegiac words of John Howland, writing about Ralph McGill in *Time*. Ralph Waldo Emerson McGill was editor, and then publisher, of the *Atlanta Constitution*, during the 1940s, 50s and 60s. He became known as the "Conscience of the South" for speaking out in the paper against social injustice. McGill publicly opposed the Ku Klux Klan and segregationist Governor Eugene Talmadge; he deplored such acts as the burning of a black school and the bombing of a Jewish temple. His stands won him a Pulitzer Prize, but advertisers in his newspaper were boycotted, and McGill was shot at and had crosses burned on his lawn.

McGill died in 1969. More than a decade later, Atlanta renamed a street bearing the name of the first Imperial Wizard of the Ku Klux Klan. The new name is Ralph McGill Boulevard.

---

know our secret signal."

His eyes were wide, and he nodded his head vigorously.

"Plus," I cautioned him solemnly, "answering the door is out of the question. If someone rings the bell, don't even go near the door. Pretend that no one's home, and they'll go away. Breakfast is cereal. Lunch is a cold sandwich. And under no circumstances are you to use the oven, the toaster or the microwave."

It was a detailed list for such a small boy but I had delivered it with an urgency that seemed to impress him.

I performed my duties in a fog. In the numbing cold, I went through the motions of weighing and marking palletized equipment and other cargo that were to be loaded on the huge waiting C130 and C141 aircraft. Then I ran inside to my computer to figure out how to arrange loads within the aircraft to balance their weight.

The hours trickled by as slowly as refrigerated molasses as I waited for my 12-hour stint to come to an end. For the fifth time that day, I called home to check in with Kharim. "Hey, little man," I greeted him, trying to keep my voice upbeat. "How is everything? Are you guys okay?"

"We're fine, Mommy," my son bravely assured me. "I did everything you said, and Kharyse even took a nap." He giggled. "We have a Christmas present waiting for you when you get home." I was proud that he seemed to have the situation firmly in hand but I still felt terrible that he had been forced to take on my adult responsibilities.

Finally, at 1630 hours, the duty day came to a close. The last aircraft had safely departed, and I could pack up my computer and head home. Using our secret signal, I called Kharim and told him I was on my way, and then I sped down Interstate 64 toward my precious babies.

Imagine my happiness as I stepped into our quarters and my children rushed into my arms. Imagine my surprise when I found the house neat, not a toy out of place. Imagine my joy when my two younger children led me over to our worn-out sofa, unlaced my boots and tugged them from my feet, then placed their small hands over my eyes to blindfold me.

Now imagine my delight when Kharim, wearing a huge grin, presented me with a Teenaged Mutant Ninja Turtle lap tray, laden with a cheese sandwich, chips and a cup of tea, made with hot water straight from the tap. Never was a Christmas dinner so lovingly prepared. And although Kharim had disobeyed my instructions and "grilled" the sandwich in the microwave, just imagine the love and pride I felt in being the mother of these three wonderful children.

Several years have passed since that Christmas, and my children and I have faced many other separations and challenges. And yes, there were other days when I wanted to give up, to sit down on my rucksack and throw my hands high in the air. But the memory of that day, engraved in my heart, kept me going.

Today, I am part of a family of eight. I have a loving husband and three more children. I'm no longer a soldier, but my days as a military mom proved to me that we'll adapt and endure. We're made of some mighty tough stuff, my family and I.

Tracy Price Thompson, a retired U.S. Army Engineer lives with her family in Fort Dix, New Jersey. A Rutgers student, her most recent novel is Black Coffee *(www.iUniverse.com).*

> *"A jug fills drop by drop."*
> —Buddha

SECTION VIII

♦ TIES THAT BIND ♦

"Perfect love casteth out fear."
—NEW TESTAMENT, 1 JOHN, IV:18

LOVE IN THE LAND OF LOSS
Caroline Leavitt

I was married in a state of terror. At the rabbi's first words, I began to sob uncontrollably. My husband-to-be took my hand and held it tight, but I wept through my wedding ceremony, crying so hard that my mascara streamed down my cheeks and my nose ran. I wept because I knew I was tempting disaster. I wept because I was waiting for the man I now loved more than life itself to die suddenly and inexplicably, just moments before we would be man and wife.

My fear was not so crazy. In 1987, two weeks before the first wedding I'd planned, my then fiancé had suffered a heart attack so massive that no miracle of modern medicine could have saved him. In shock, I had spent nearly two years roaming the country, traveling away from my grief.

When my money ran out, I returned to New York and sought comfort in a young widows' support group. There were 10 women in it, ages 18 to 40. They sat beside me on plush couches and made me fragrant herbal tea. They rubbed the tension from my shoulders and stroked my hair. And then, to my absolute horror, they told me, with great assurance: "You will never have love like you had before. You will always be damaged."

I lasted a month in this group. But even out of the group, I kept hearing their voices, a Greek chorus of despair.

I was desperate to prove that I could be happy again, that life could go on. And so a few months later, I began to date. But nothing took. Eventually I spent a year with a man with whom I had nothing in common, purely out of fear of being alone with my misery. "You have no ability to love," he informed me coolly when he left me. I suspected that he might be right.

Finally, a friend insisted I meet someone she swore I'd like. His name was Jeff. He was 38, an editor and writer, smart and funny and handsome. And my friend was right. I did like him, so hard and so fast that I was torn between relief and fear.

"So," I said casually, on one of our first dates. "Any incidence of heart problems in your family?" Amused, patient, and knowing something about my past, he offered to show me his bill of health. But finding out that he was healthy didn't calm me for, to my utter astonishment, I was falling in love—and love in my experience meant loss. Remembering all those young widows, stubborn and stuck in their pasts, I told myself I could be different. Love might last this time, if only I were brave enough to chance it.

Two years later, I finally found the courage to play it unsafe and get married. Newly wed, I tried to relax. But I woke up nights to watch Jeff breathe. When he was ten minutes late, I panicked. I kept waiting for the other shoe to drop.

"There is no other shoe," Jeff insisted.

Ah, but then I became pregnant.

I was strong and in good health, and I had a topnotch obstetrician. I took extra care. I had every prenatal test. I called my doctor at the slightest twinge. I felt so healthy and happy that I began to tell myself, *Everything is alright.*

I not only read every baby book I could get my hands on, I memorized chapters. And I bonded with the baby, massaging my belly, showering with love what was little more than a speed bump of a boy. When my son grew big enough to be able to detect sound from the womb, I spoke to him constantly, and sang the Beatles' *I Will,* chosen because I loved the affirmation. "I will, I will, I will," I repeated like a mantra.

Max was a C-section. I lay with my arms strapped to a table, waiting, anxious, woozy from the anesthesia. Beside me, in green scrubs, Jeff held my hands. When Jeff burst into tears, I felt a

Legend of a Faithful Wife

Odysseus, Greek king of the island of Ithaca, was married for only a year when he went off to fight in the Trojan War, leaving behind his cherished wife Penelope and their infant son Telemachus. It was a long war and a longer return. During Odysseus's 17-year absence, Penelope never lost hope that he was alive and would return. However, everyone else believed Odysseus long dead.

About 100 of the young lords of Ithaca and the surrounding islands had taken residence at Odysseus's palace, intent on persuading Penelope to marry one of them, who could then lay claim to the kingdom. These suitors gave themselves the run of the palace, slaughtering the king's livestock for their drunken feasts, drinking his casks of wine and rudely ordering his servants about.

Fearful, yet determined to hold the nobles at bay, Penelope came up with a cunning plan. "You are right," she announced to her uninvited guests. "It is time for me to remarry. However, when I do so I shall be leaving these halls, and my elderly father-in-law, Laertes, will have no woman to care for him. Before I remarry I must weave for him a funeral shroud, for I should dishonor him and disgrace myself if he were to die and be buried without one."

After three years, the shroud was nowhere near completion. For day after day, Penelope sat at her loom, weaving; and night after night, she unraveled her day's work. This stratagem worked quite well until one of Penelope's maids betrayed her mistress's secret to the suitors.

Enraged, the would-be bridegrooms demanded that Penelope quit stalling. By now, even her own parents were pressuring her to make her choice and remarry. The embattled Penelope, inspired by the gods, proposed a most challenging contest of skill to help her choose: She would give her hand to the man who could string Odysseus's bow and shoot an arrow through the holes in the heads of twelve battle axes.

Twelve axes were fetched and set upright in a row, so that the holes in the backs of the axe-heads were perfectly aligned. A bow that Odysseus had left behind was brought in. One by one the suit-

ors attempted to bend the bow in order to string it, and one by one, they failed. Suddenly an old beggar, stooped and dressed in rags, emerged from the crowd. "Kindly allow me to try," he requested. "I should like to see if anything remains of the strength I had as a young man." Despite the suitors' jeers, the bow was handed over to the beggar, who easily bent the bow, fit the string in the notch of the bow, and sent an arrow whizzing straight and true through the holes in the axe-heads.

The beggar then announced his identity: He was the returned Odysseus, disguised in order to take vengeance on the nobles who had invaded his halls and tormented his wife. After slaying the suitors, he took back his rightful place as Ithaca's ruler and Penelope's mate. Penelope's endurance was rewarded at last.

clip of fear. "Something's wrong," I thought. And I knew what it was: The other shoe. A stiletto. A steel-toed boot. And then I looked up, and there was our son. He was like moonlight. His eyes were wide open and when they met mine, a constellation opened up inside of me. I fell in love. Then I shut my eyes, and my whole life changed.

This is what I remember. Waking up in a hospital bed with a strange doctor hovering over me. "You've been comatose for two weeks," he said. I watched the doctor's mouth moving, forming words. "We nearly lost you. You have a Factor Eight Inhibitor. You've been very sick, but we think you're going to be just fine."

"Where's my son?" I said.

But the doctor kept talking, telling me about the condition that kept my blood from clotting, the four operations it had taken to stop my bleeding, the continuing treatments.

"Where's Max?" I asked. "Where's Jeff?"

"Your whole family was here," the doctor said. "From Boston. From Maryland. Your friends. Every day."

"Where?" I whispered. "When?" I tried to pull myself up, and the room narrowed into black.

Time stretched like elastic. I hallucinated on morphine. Doctors with cement blocks for heads came in and out of the room. Next to me was a woman in a blue and white dotted-Swiss party dress, tied to a wheelchair, with a combination safe over her head. Panicked, I spotted a nurse and grabbed for her.

"Call my husband," I begged.

"Why, honey, he was just here."

I began to rant. The nurse was lying to me. I fell back onto the bed, suddenly cold with fear. "Are he and the baby dead?" I asked.

"Honey," the nurse soothed. "They're alive. It's just the medication making you think such things."

A week passed. And then another. And then I was waking from a dream, aware that someone was holding my hand. As I opened my eyes, Jeff's face swam into focus, and I burst into tears. "You're alive," I said in amazement. I reached out to touch him, to make him real, and then I couldn't let go. "Is Max alive?"

He kissed my fingers. "Of course he is. He's beautiful. It's too infectious here for him to visit. He's at home with the baby nurse."

When Jeff finally left, two hours past visiting hours, he told me he'd call as soon as he got home. "I have a surprise for you."

I couldn't sleep after he left. At first, I kept replaying his visit. And then, as the hospital began to quiet down for the night, I began to imagine disaster. Car accidents. Random acts of God. I sat up, panicking, and then the phone rang.

"I told you I'd call. Hang on. Someone wants to talk to you." Suddenly there was babbling, soft and high-pitched. "Say hi to your son," Jeff said.

I bolted upright in bed. I held the receiver so close to my ear it left marks. And then I began to talk to my son, to tell him how sorry I was to have missed his first six weeks, how I would make it up to him. "Max," I said. "It's Mommy."

The next day, Jeff began to bring in photos of Max, taping them everywhere, so that no matter where I looked, I'd see Max. He brought in a home movie, and the nurses wheeled me into their training room so I could watch my son in his first bath, in his stroller. We watched the film three times, and that night was the first time since I'd been in the hospital that I slept through the night.

The more Jeff visited, the more photos and tapes he inundated me with, the better I felt. "Blood count's up," the doctor told me. "We're all really pleased." The he broke into a grin. "You're well enough now so that Max can come visit you."

I was as anxious as if I were going on a blind date. I made Jeff go out and buy eyeliner, eye shadow, mascara, and lipstick. I wanted a new hairbrush and tiny gold earrings. "Will he know me?" I kept asking; but what I was thinking was: "Will he like me?"

The morning of Max's visit, I woke at five. I gathered up my supplies and hobbled to the bathroom. I couldn't stand without leaning against the sink, and my hands shook. I applied my makeup. I brushed my long hair. When I got back into bed it was only 5:15.

At nine in the morning, I was wheeled into the solarium. Jeff was smiling at me, and in his arms was Max. "I'd know you anywhere," I said, taking Max in my arms. But he strained against me, reaching for Jeff. "Look at Mommy," Jeff coaxed, and Max began to wail. Desperate, I did the only thing I could think to do. I began to sing *I Will,* our bonding song.

Max quieted. "Look," Jeff said in a hushed voice. There was no sound except for my raspy voice. There was no motion except for my arms, rocking my own, my baby, my son.

Two weeks later, I was well enough to come home to my family.

Now every morning before Max wakes, I stand in front of the mirror, staring at my ruined body, a map of stitches, bandaged in gauze. And then Jeff comes in with Max and kisses my face. "You are beautiful," he says. "And I am insane with love."

They say that after a forest fire, new growth flourishes, fertilized by the ashes of the trees destroyed. My happiness these days is like that, pushing up exuberantly from loss, strengthened by pain. Life is a risky business. But I'm alive and healthy. And because I fought my fear and gave my heart again, I have a husband and a baby. I'm loved. I get to have this, I keep telling myself in wonder. And then what I feel most is blessed.

Caroline Leavitt is the award-winning author of six novels; the most recent is Living Other Lives. *She lives in Hoboken, New Jersey. This story is adapted from a version that appeared in* A Few Thousand Words about Love, *edited by Mickey Pearlman (St. Martin's Press, 1997).*

TRIUMPH OF A TODDLER
Malinda Teel

Around the time he turned two, my son Sam showed a blossoming awareness of the social niceties. "Sank oo," he would say when I got him a cup of apple juice. "No, sank oo," he would demur, when I offered him a serving of broccoli. Sometimes he would even say "pwease."

It was about this time that I made one of my sporadic efforts to interest him in his potty, which had ornamented our bathroom for some months. Sam lay wriggling on a changing pad, and as I struggled to fasten safety pins in a clean diaper without impaling his tender flesh, I broached the subject in a tone of voice calculated to be casual. "You know, you could sit on the potty when you make a poop. Mommy will be glad to help you if you let me know when you need to go."

Gazing up at me from his supine position, Sam briefly considered the idea. "No, sank oo," he responded.

We had bought the potty chair earlier in the year, on Bastille Day. Whether it was Sam's independence or my own I was looking forward to, I do not remember. What I do know is that my chest grew a bit tight every time I anticipated the process of toilet training my first (and only) child. On the scale of parenting challenges, it seemed to loom right up there next to Getting Through the Teenage Years. I had read enough Freudian theory to know that in persuading my son to trade in his diaper for those cute little big-boy pants in the superhero print, I held his future mental health in my hands. If I were overly eager, pushing him before he had gained the necessary muscular control or cooperative spirit, he could become a tense, miserly, rigid adult, withholding of both affection and money. If I somehow missed the cues that he was ready for the transition, I could undermine

his feelings of competence for life. The mess in his diaper could somehow be transmogrified into messy relationships, messy work habits, a messy existence. Timing was everything. And I wasn't so sure my sense of timing was reliable.

When we bought the potty, I knew that Sam, at 20 months, might be too young to use it. All the baby-book gurus said so, including Dr. Spock. But they seemed to think it was a good idea to have a potty hanging around, to let the child become familiar with it. And besides, I wanted to be prepared.

Sam did show some initial interest in the thing. He used it, with the lid closed, as a chair. He scooted it over to the sink and used it as a step stool. But after a couple weeks, he abruptly grew bored with it and ignored it altogether. Periodically—but not too frequently, I hoped—I would reintroduce the subject of its use, suppressing my anxiety about inflicting emotional scars on his vulnerable psyche. "Why don't you try sitting on your potty while I read you a story?" I might suggest, as if a wonderful inspiration had just hit me.

Sam wasn't buying it. As the months rolled by and we approached the anniversary of our purchase of the potty, I began to grow fretful. I wanted this milestone behind us, so that I could look back and know we had not lost our way on this particular developmental path. I soothed my nerves by reminding myself that no kindergartner had ever entered the local elementary school with a supply of Pampers in his backpack.

And then one evening, several hours after one of my potty pep talks, Sam surprised me by asking that I remove his diaper so he could sit on the potty.

Although he remained seated long enough for the potty to emboss his bottom with a circular red mark, not much else happened. Nonetheless, I began to feel hopeful.

Three days later, just as I was about to hustle him out the door to preschool, Sam again requested—no, insisted—that he use the potty. After 15 minutes the potty was still empty. "Sweetie, we're late for school, I prompted him."

"No, no, I not ready," he pleaded tearfully. At last I persuaded him to discontinue his effort by suggesting we take the potty with us to preschool.

And then, back at home that afternoon, it happened. After Sam's nap, I noticed him tensing his body in that telltale way. "Why don't you go sit on the potty?" I suggested. "Unh-unh," he said, shaking his head no. "Come on, your body is telling you it's time," I gently encouraged, taking his hand. He allowed himself to be led to the bathroom, and this time his attempt met with success. I felt like breaking out the champagne but confined myself to warm (but moderated) congratulations. ("Don't make too big a deal of it," warn the baby books.) Inwardly I was cheering.

UNLEARNING HELPLESSNESS

P sychologists are not always very nice people. A long time ago a few of them were studying motivation. They put two groups of mice (I'd rather it was rats) into a challenging situation. It consisted of giving them a shock and watching them try to escape. Only half of them had a place to escape to; the other half had no place to go. Next they put all of them into a vat of water and watched them swim until they drowned. (I warned you about psychologists!) The top swimmers averaged 60 hours. But those who had already experienced powerlessness in the face of adversity were found to have learned helplessness: They did not swim nearly as long as the others before giving their lives for science.

Children are accidentally learning helplessness or mastery all the time. Then they grow up to be us. We are all some version of the mouse that couldn't get away. But there's a great lesson for us here: Just because we can't do a thing doesn't necessarily mean it's impossible for us. Maybe we've only learned to believe that it's impossible. How can we ever be sure if we don't test ourselves?

There are any number of ways to test our human limits, from starting a business to mountain climbing. The bicycle racer pushing down the pedal one more time as he battles up the hill is finding the edge of what he is capable of. That's a big part of why he does it. At some point he will no longer be able to move forward. If his body and his will fail simultaneously, he has already won the important race—the one with himself. For another person, a health problem might provide the challenge to give her personal best. Family, work, school, and just living test us all the time. Every second contains a challenge to be all that we can be.

Life is our swimming vat—and, true, we will all eventually drown. But what we do on the way down—and how we test ourselves—is what life is all about.

Nietzsche said, "What doesn't destroy me, makes me stronger." We enter life with undifferentiated potential, like a block of granite ready for the sculptor. As we meet life's challenges, we carve our character, defining ourselves in clean-edged detail. If, with courage, we continue chipping away at the rough edges to reveal the best we are capable of, we just may find we've created a work of art.

I wouldn't want to live a life without challenge. At 66, I stay pretty active. I'm just in from working on my camper. In a matter of weeks I'll be driving from the East Coast to New Mexico, where I'll be climbing around on an 11,000-foot mountain, seeking to bring down a 1,000-pound elk, with a bow. I lift weights almost daily and play squash just as often. There will be time for me to take my 27-foot sailboat out for a few races before I leave. Did I mention that I have fibromyalgia, sleep problems and that I just finished a year of cancer treatment?

If you haven't challenged yourself, start now. It doesn't have to be elaborate. Hold a quart of milk out at arm's length and time yourself. When you realize that you can improve on this, freedom begins. Decide to do something difficult and do it. You'll swim longer.

—Dick Marron

Dick Marron is a family therapist and was in private practice for 20 years. He lives in Connecticut, in the house his grandfather built, and is a great-grandfather.

I cheered too soon. The event I had hoped was a harbinger of change turned out to be a one-shot deal. Days passed into weeks, and Sam remained intransigent in his refusal to use the contraption again. "Where did I go wrong?" I began to ask myself. I turned to his teachers at the preschool for advice.

"Don't worry about it," said Suzanne. "Both my children were over three when they were trained." I quickly did the math in my head, and discovered with a mixture of relief and agony that this gave me another half-year.

"I remember what a hard time I had with my son," sympathized Lynn. "He was so afraid of failing."

Boing. It hit me! I had been so focused on acquitting myself honorably on this proving ground that I'd been oblivious to the possibility that giving up his diapers might require courage of Sam. It was all very well for his sphincter muscles to be sufficiently developed; he still would have to take that leap of faith essential to all brave new ventures. Compassion filled my heart like a sunrise.

Within three months, Sam had graduated to training pants. It's not that I did anything terribly different but I'm sure I relaxed some. And Sam, bit by bit, opened himself to my encouragement, until his pride in his successes outweighed his ambivalence. The timing, finally, was right, physically and emotionally.

Though toilet training may seem an unlikely vehicle for enlightenment, this is what I learned from the experience: My child does not need for me to know all the answers in advance. He needs for me to stick by him and keep trying. He needs for me to believe in him.

And he needs for me to remember that growing up, like parenting, is a journey filled with fearsome challenges and calls to persevere.

THE FIRST YEAR
Anne Tucker

My boyfriend, Alan, was wonderful. As good-looking as a film star, he was a stranger to vanity. On top of that, he was outgoing and generous and had a wry sense of humor that impressed both my friends and parents. "This is a man you could live with," my mom said.

But Alan had one characteristic that unnerved me: He was a neatnik. His dress shirts, expertly ironed and folded at a Chinese laundry, were perfectly stacked on the closet shelves of his bachelor apartment. Every surface in the place was clear of debris. His kitchen was immaculate.

Before we married, I never mentioned to Alan that his pursuit of flawless order bothered me. Cleanliness is next to godliness, right? Commenting would have exposed my inner slob, something I was loathe to do while auditioning for the role of partner.

Alan, of course, had visited the studio apartment I shared with a friend, and he had never said anything about the clutter there. Maybe he assumed it was my roommate's mess, since I emulated his neatness when I was at his place.

As time passed, however, the disparity in our natures became more evident. I liked windows wide open, for example, while he preferred them closed, warning me that the sill was a dirt collector. When I cooked, I endeavored to clean as I went along—something I'd never done before—but he re-scrubbed mixing bowls that had already passed through my soapy hands. I felt reproached, but had to admit he did the better job.

In those dating days of wine and rose-colored glasses, I put the best construction on Alan's ways. But after we married and moved into a fifth-floor flat, some old saws about marriage turned out to be true. Our best behavior slipped away, and yes, the first year was, in some respects, the hardest. We cleaned the apartment together on Saturdays but I dropped the pretense of trying to keep up with him in the Good Housekeeping sweep-stakes as he tidied up daily.

His military training showed in the precision with which he made the bed. The sheets were so taut that I could not easily slide between them. I didn't whine about this; instead, I made a great show of kicking them loose.

I tended to read three or four magazines or books at a time. I'd leave them open on my night table or dog-eared on the couch or on the bathroom floor. If Alan picked up one in my presence to restore it to a shelf, he might ask, "Is this yours?"

Who else's could it be?

I might protest that I was just about to read the offending publication, or promise to put it away later—although we both knew that "later" rarely came. What really irked me, however, was when Alan straightened up the place when I was out. A crossword I hadn't finished would be gone forever; a cookbook would be stashed on a shelf I could reach only by standing on a chair. Or, running late, I'd grab for a canvas bag I'd left hanging on a doorknob two days earlier, only to realize it had, no doubt, been neatly folded and put *where?*

We joked about our differences in front of friends, but we never discussed with each other our disagreement about order and disorder, which was rapidly becoming a metaphor for control versus autonomy. Each of us secretly thought he or she was exhibiting exemplary fortitude in tolerating the other person's idiosyncrasies.

The battle royale came six months into our marriage, sparked by a Comet can. I always left the cleanser and sponge on the bathtub ledge, so I could scrub away the tub ring while I was still wet. Alan dared complain about this handy arrangement while

we were cleaning one Saturday, saying there was a disgusting rust imprint on the tub rim.

One word led to another until there were dozens of angry words flying through our bedroom, followed by the can of Comet, which I hurled at Alan, who was standing in front of a large window. The cleanser sailed through the window, which (Alan's preference) was closed at the time. Fortunately, the can didn't bean anyone before crashing in the street and being squashed by a car. The glazier's bill busted that week's budget.

We were chastened but nothing had been resolved. I'd like to

A BRAVE ROMANCE

W hen Elizabeth Barrett left her family's London house one sunny September morning in 1846, she had scarcely slept a wink the night before. She was bound for Marylebone Church and her own secret wedding to the poet, Robert Browning. As she and her maid, Wilson, proceeded down the street, Elizabeth staggered. Wilson, fearful that her mistress might faint, hurried her to a pharmacy, where smelling salts revived her.

Elizabeth certainly had more reason for anxiety than most brides, for at age 40, she was making a choice that would likely cost her father's love. During their courtship, Elizabeth had often expressed fears to Robert about how her father might react if he discovered their love. "I shall be killed—it will be so infinitely worse than you can have an idea," she wrote in one note.

Elizabeth's courage in loving Robert went beyond risking her father's wrath. In opening herself to this relationship, she had to defy her own ideas about who she was and what life held for her. When Robert introduced himself to Elizabeth by letter in January of 1845, she was a published poet of some repute. However, she was a semi-invalid, confining herself much of the time to a couch in her room, where she lived a life of the mind, reading and writing. For years she had suffered from respiratory ailments and heart irregularities, and her strength was further debilitated by inactivity and such unhealthy habits as drinking nothing but strong black coffee.

She was also painfully shy and avoided face-to-face contacts with people outside the family. Behind this shyness lay a fear of rejection. As she later wrote to Robert, "I never thought that anyone whom I could love would stoop to love me." Furthermore, Elizabeth had been devastated by the unexpected deaths of her mother and two brothers and feared that if she allowed herself too much happiness, fate might snatch it away. All in all, she seemed to view infirmity and secluded spinsterhood as her lot in life.

Then she received a passionately admiring letter from Robert who, although he'd never seen her, declared, "I love your verses with all my heart, dear Miss Barrett . . . and I love you too."

Elizabeth wrote to a friend, "I had a letter from Browning the poet last night, which threw me into ecstasies." The correspondence between the two flourished, and Robert patiently wooed Elizabeth with discussions of poetry. Finally she found the courage to allow him to visit. The sound of his footsteps on the stairs as he approached her room the first time caused her heart to beat as wildly as a trapped animal's—but the visit went well.

By fall, Elizabeth and Robert were emphatically in love. As another year passed, their love grew, as did Elizabeth's stamina, and she and Robert made plans to marry and move to Italy, where the warmer climate might benefit Elizabeth's health. Shortly before their marriage, she wrote of finding the will to leave her little room forever: "I have none in the world who will hold me to make me live in it, except only you. I have come back for you alone."

After Elizabeth and Robert set out for Italy, her father did indeed disown her; he returned her letters unopened. Although this was a continuing sorrow to Elizabeth, she never regretted her decision. She and Robert had a son together, and their love endured until Elizabeth's death at 55.

tell you we quietly talked over our underlying issues, but that didn't happen. Instead, Alan retreated behind a mask of elaborate courtesy because he was afraid of me. I was afraid of me, too. And although I loved him, I was worried that our happy marriage was a facade. But every time that incubus of a thought popped into my mind, I'd punch it down and focus on something else.

A few days before Alan's 26th birthday, I found him a gift in a flea market, a pair of lapis-inlaid sterling cufflinks that would look terrific with the shirts he wore to his buttoned-down job. The seller folded them in a piece of old newspaper, which he stuck into a worn yellow plastic bag.

I left my purchase on my bureau to remind me to buy a box and ribbon. A couple of evenings later I came home with the wrappings, only to discover the plastic bag gone. Alan, mistaking it for trash, had tossed it down the incinerator.

This time, I didn't get mad; I got sad, and sobbed out the truth of my feelings. My husband listened and talked about his. As we began to understand one another, Alan opened a window to let in fresh air.

Now that we've been married over two decades and have three children, I see that incident as a defining moment, a new beginning. But our ability to endure wasn't built on that or any other single day. True fortitude in marriage means hanging in there for the long haul, and finding ways to respect both your own needs and those of your partner. Once trust becomes a habit, a dirty coffee cup is a dirty coffee cup, not a symbol of a frightening lack of self-discipline. And the query, "Are you reading this book?" is a sincere question, not a shaming technique.

The odd thing is that these days I'm probably a bit neater than Alan is. The change began when our first two children were very young. In those busy, sleep-deprived days, I learned to make lists and put objects where they belonged in order to survive. And Alan instinctively knew that a toddler who wanted help with his blocks took precedence over an eat-on kitchen floor. Some chores waited weeks to get done or were accomplished hastily and ineptly, and the sun rose daily as our little guys sloshed cereal on themselves. Alan relaxed, and found he enjoyed it.

Anne Tucker is a New York publicist.

AMOS, A WILD CAT
Clarice Belcher

I first met Amos when he was 1 1/2 years old. He was in the cat section of the humane shelter, cramped in a metal cage, a beautiful orange tabby of Abyssinian and Somalian descent. It was his Somalian ancestry that gave him his flirty dandelion tail.

I'd wanted a pet to ease the pain of a two-year relationship that was ending and had called the shelter to order the cat I desired: one tabby, please, neutered and declawed, to go. But now, presented with what I'd asked for, I felt a rising apprehension. It had been a long time since I'd had an animal in my life. And I'd been used to dogs, big dogs, like St. Bernards and Newfoundlands. I wasn't sure I knew what to do with a cat. As Amos fixed his celery green eyes on mine, I felt apprehensive.

The shelter assistant removed Amos from his cage. "Would you like to hold him?" she asked, placing him carefully in my arms. Amos leaned his body into mine. He felt soft and warm and still, like a napping infant.

"Oh, my," I said, feeling his silky fur, "he certainly is wonderful." Torn by uncertainty, I asked, "Could you hold him one more day while I think about it?"

"Yes," the assistant replied, "but just for a day."

That night, at home alone, I weighed my anxiety about getting Amos against the warmth I'd known in holding him in my arms. The warmth won.

I brought him home on February the 14th—Valentine's Day. I held him close, his paws kneading my chest. I imagined a life of bliss. I ended up with a life in hell.

It turned out that Amos was a biter. And the person he was biting was me.

It was nothing serious at first, just the occasional nip on my ankle or hand. But then the nips turned into full-fledged attacks. The worst of these attacks occurred over an orange chair in my home office. It was his favorite seat.

Amos was resting in that chair one day, curled into the shape of a Q, his tail dangling over the upholstered seat. As I picked him up to move him so that I could use the chair, he suddenly bit my forearm. I straightened up and screamed, dropping him. Amos crouched on the floor, eerily still.

I stared at his tense body and glazed eyes. Slowly I lowered myself into the chair. With every hair erect, Amos vaulted over the arm of the chair and bit me again, right on the shoulder. His paws hit the floor—*thump, thump*—and he scurried out of the room. I sat in a daze, blood trickling from the puncture wounds left by his bites. Terrified, I felt like a captive in my own home, the hostage of an eight-pound cat.

In tears, I called my vet. "Cat bites are dangerous," he warned me. "If this continues, you may have to consider putting Amos to sleep."

Stunned, I plopped down in the orange chair.

I didn't want to put Amos to sleep. I loved him.

Passionate and most times unflappable, he was like a swash-buckling pirate. He strutted around my apartment like a feline Errol Flynn, his hind legs trousered in orange fur that billowed like bloomers. He was the only cat I knew who put out fires. Whenever I lit a candle, as I often did when I wrote in my jour-nal, he'd hunker down and move in close. With quick, crisp taps of his paw, he'd snuff the candle out. Then he'd swagger across the pages of my notebook, lie down near the edge of my desk, and lick his waxy paw with a flourish. And, unlike most cats, he was kind to plants, leaving my ferns and philodendrons intact in their pots.

A cat of such distinction deserved better than death. I made a list of the things I could try to cure him of his biting. I started by consulting animal healers—gentle women offering kindness and 17 essential herbs. I religiously sprinkled their remedies on Amos and his food, like a priest flicking holy water. I was crushed when he bit me four times in one week.

I scratched the healers' names off the list and moved on to books and health food stores. I studied cat diets. I plied him with organic foods and tiny bits of chicken and raw fish. I was devastated when he bit me three times in three days.

In desperation, I dosed him with catnip to get him into a harness to walk off his energy. But the catnip wore off, Amos escaped, and I spent two hours chasing after him. I caught him, he bit me, and I ended up with a tetanus shot.

For months I searched for ways to cure him, but nothing worked. I became increasingly anxious, fearful as I turned corners in my own home that I would find Amos waiting, ready to strike.

I pulled out my list for the final time. There at the bottom was the name of a holistic veterinarian. I called for a visit, hoping she might recommend some miracle potion. During our appointment, she asked simply, "Does he get out often?"

"Never, " I replied. "He has no front claws, no outdoor defenses."

"I think he needs to get out," she said, and she showed me a picture of a cat playpen. It was the shape and size of a 1920s icebox with wheels. I studied its black-finished metal and wire mesh and began to think of it as a screened porch—cat-sized, just right for Amos.

I looked at the price and gasped. As clearly as if the cat porch were labeled "Last Chance," I knew I'd reached my limit. I'd buy the play pen, but it would be the last thing I'd buy.

On the day it arrived, I assembled it quickly. When I had snapped the last piece in place, I threw in handfuls of catnip and eased Amos in, closing the metal door. I rolled him across the soft, carpeted floor to the back porch door. Then I rolled him over the concrete slab; the wheels grated noisily against the bumpy surface. All the while, Amos sat still on the plastic floor of his porch, facing forward, his eyes wide with wonder.

Outside, he paced from one end of his porch to the other, his ears rotating forward and backward, listening to cawing crows, children's squeals faint in the distance, cars on asphalt roads, footsteps on a nearby sidewalk. He sniffed at the aromas of food wafting from my Asian and Spanish neighbors' kitchens, their fragrance carried on the back of a breeze that lightly ruffled his fur. Warmed by the summer sun, he studied the yard, the trees, and the sky with quiet and inquisitive dignity, king of the back porch and beyond.

I sipped my tea quietly, sitting in silence with Amos in the calm of that restful afternoon.

From that day on, his biting ceased. We live happily together now, Amos and I, but I sometimes wonder about those earlier times. The day that I brought him home, I thought it was I who was giving him his chance. But maybe it was he who was giving me mine—to experience the reward that only enduring for love can bring.

Clarice L. Belcher is a writer and teacher and is currently pursuing her interest in the healing arts. She lives in Atlanta, Georgia, and is owned by her cat, Amos.

WAKE-UP CALL
T. J. Elliott

I   t is 5:15 AM. I am 13 years old. My father pushes open the door to my bedroom and says simply but forcefully, "UP!" If this had been one of his whimsical mornings, he might have repeated the word again and again, like some chant of exhortation. There are the mornings when he is a drill instructor and the mornings when he is a coach, or an opera singer or a Shakespearean actor. But this is his minimalist morning: one breath and one bark.

I know that I must respond quickly. If my feet do not instantly hit the floor, he will commence conversation. I don't want conversation. If my father realizes, as he clatters about the kitchen, that I have not moved toward the bathroom, he will return to my room to dog my every stride, in order to guard against any lapse into relaxation. My father will push and pull me into another day. He is getting me up.

I am the youngest of his five sons; my little sister, the Princess, completes the family. My father got us all up, always. Every morning. He did not trust alarm clocks or our resolve. He was determined that we would get where we were supposed to go, and get there on time.

And we were supposed to be going somewhere. That was the point. Track practice, part-time job, debating meet, Scout trip, and most of all, school. His push in the morning, literal or figurative, was intended to propel us into some enterprise, some undertaking that transformed us mentally or spiritually or physically. Emotions, I guess, we could attend to on our own time.

Dad relished those moments of awakening. He made them rituals and celebrations. When I was very young, his routine of rousing my brothers excited me also. I endeavored to rise as early as my father so that I could stand by him at the door to their room. He encouraged me to make noise. I would mimic a trumpet by cupping one hand and blowing out my cheeks to blare a version of reveille through my lips. On some days, he coaxed me to sing *McNamara's Band* or *Yankee Doodle Dandy*, as laughs rolled out of him and my brothers groaned. Of course, my turn would come, but this was the 1950s and I had no concept of karma.

My father was never late, in my memory. No sick days, no mornings off. He most often appeared at our bedroom doors already shaved, hair combed back, wearing a white V-neck undershirt and slate gray suit pants that my mother pressed sharp. (The coffee cup in his hand was for delivery to her; she didn't do the dawn patrol.) A big man with a booming voice, he was aware of his size, aware of his deep, thunderous tone. Often I opened my eyes to those bare powerful arms and hands spread wide over me, then swinging together in an ear-splitting clap. And sometimes before I even gained my vision, I'd hear him reciting sonorous poems like *The Charge of the Light Brigade* or *The Hound of Heaven*. He exhorted us with his whole being to listen, to learn, to think, to seize this day and all the others coming.

We did not always return this passion. He, however, would not give up on us, even when we wanted to give up on some commitment. For example, impressed by incense and Church Latin and black cassocks, all of my brothers and I in turn signed up to be altar boys at daily mass. I signed up in September, and the nuns trained me when mornings were still warm and there was light even on the way to 7 o'clock mass. I did not think of January then. But when we eventually tired of the routine, my father would not let us quit. He stood us up and steered us to the bathroom sink, if necessary. He made sure we showed up.

This was not gentle. Gentle, I think, would not have worked;

our souls were too wild. That wildness may have come from him, a mercurial man who could growl and grin all in the time that it took a boy to turn the wrong way getting out of that bed. The way he dealt with us in the mornings was the way he dealt with life: purposeful, energetic, and fierce. He hung a carving of Aesop's grasshopper and the busy ants atop our bathroom mirror. The inscription said, "The world owes you a living but you have to work hard to collect it." We did not need the carving to divine his philosophy.

Imagine this awakening every morning. Every morning. He came home from World War II and before long was calling my eldest brother to breakfast and school. He worked as a short order cook at Nathan's in Times Square and studied electrical engineering at night. Still, he got us up and graduated near the top of his class; he had four kids by then. He kept getting us up while he started his own business, abandoning a comfortable office and a company car to sell his products to machine shops out of an old station wagon. Soon, he was turning us all out of bed to pile drowsily into that Chrysler station wagon and head off to the dusty warehouse he rented. John, Jimmy, Michael, Brendan, T. J., and Irene, we all swept the floors, packed boxes, answered phones. He taught us how to work. And he taught us that getting up was the first part of the job.

As my brothers and I went to high school, the hour of rising edged earlier. When I chose a Jesuit school almost 60 miles from our new home, he did not hesitate, although he must have known that the task of rousing a teenage boy at five every morning is not a blessing. I caught the 6:04 train that first year. (Later, he would relent to the 6:16 and then, when I was a senior, to the luxurious 6:33.) Each morning, he summoned his old short-order skills and scrambled eggs around whatever was left over from the previous night's dinner. The result was not culinary art, but it fortified me for the long day ahead. Then he added conversation to the dish: How would I translate a line of Latin stuck in his head? What did I think they were getting at by having me read Maugham? What was I after in all of this? In those adolescent morns, it was not enough to get my body up; he started working on my mind as well.

Now I have children of my own to awaken. Working at my computer or lingering over the morning newspaper as new dawns arrive, I stir against the tidal pull of the self. As I stand up from my own concerns to face the moans and grumbles of drowsy daughters, I reconsider what drives such a seemingly ordinary task. I apprehend my father in a deeper, more intricate way.

No boy appreciates his father until the day he himself is responsible for someone or something: a job, a marriage, a child. Then perhaps he knows that every morning is a choice. He recognizes all of the choices already made and understands all those nudges and shoves along the way as a single force seeking some "right direction." He can attribute to himself all that he is. Or he can admit and admire the fortitude of a father who chose again and again and again to stick with his son, to put the boy's growth ahead of the man's comfort.

Oh, this seems a simple thing: to awaken your children in the morning—laughable really in its commonness. Next to wonderful stories of climbing mountains, besting monsters, and mastering the universe, it is plain. But my whole life through, especially in the hopeless dark of wintry mornings, I keep feeling gratitude for the father with the simple strength to wake me up.

T. J. Elliott is 48 years old and lives in Tarrytown, New York with his wife, Marjorie, and their three children. He is vice-president of the consulting firm, Cavanaugh Leahy & Company.

HONORING MOTHER
Tarzie Hart

I would sit at my little school desk and squirm, perspiration beading my upper lip, on days when I was expected to get up and talk before the class. My stomach would be in knots, and my head would hurt as if a belt were being tightened around it.

Each year, the desks got bigger, and my dread of speaking in front of the class grew more unbearable. My mother would try to bolster my self-confidence. "You can do it! Just be yourself, and you'll do fine," she'd say. But her advice never helped.

Of course, public speaking didn't bother Mother one bit. She spoke extemporaneously with ease and aplomb. She taught Bible classes for years and relished opportunities to speak out against social wrongs. On one such occasion, she was serving on a jury that had found a young vagrant guilty of petty theft. The judge had given the man a jail sentence and was about to adjourn, when Mother stood up and requested permission to address the court. "With all due respect, Your Honor," she stated, "sending this man to jail and releasing him back onto the streets, still without a home, without a job, and without one dollar in his pocket, is like putting a Band Aid on an amputation." For ten minutes she held forth eloquently. When she sat back down, the other members of the jury broke into applause; and the judge pronounced that, upon release from jail, the defendant would be offered temporary employment with the County.

Mother was a wonderful Southwestern woman. She was strong, funny, tough, practical, yet very romantic. My brother and sister and I were the luckiest kids in the world to be raised by such a woman. Getting us to bed at nine like other neighborhood children was not nearly as important to her as lying with us on a blanket in the middle of our sandy west-Texas front yard. As we looked up at the billions of blazing stars and planets, she would point out all the constellations, telling us the myths that explained their names.

She was my best girlfriend, my mentor, my shoulder to cry on, my toughest critic and a part of my heart. As the years quickly passed, we grew ever closer, and I was fortunate to live near her even into my middle age.

I distinctly remember the day she called me with the chilling request to "please come down and feel this strange lump in my abdomen." As if it were yesterday, I remember holding her hand as we waited for the results of the tests that told us she had ovarian cancer.

Mother underwent chemotherapy, putting up a good fight, but the cancer eventually won. Her last days were at home, with hospice services and my sister and me there to administer morphine as often as the law would allow. Never have I felt so helpless and alone. The person I usually turned to for support in times of trouble was lying before me in misery, laboring to die on a rented hospital bed.

Caring hospice staff told us that by discontinuing IV nutrition and water, we could save our mother many days of unspeakable pain, and so we cut off her water supply—the hardest decision I have ever made. In her final hours, morphine and ice were her friends. We made hundreds of trips to her side to slip a sliver of ice between her dry and cracking lips. Otherwise, the only comforts we could offer were the sounds of our voices, offering words of love; and a CD of Kenny G's Christmas music, which she asked us to play over and over again.

The hospice staff had given us general information about the process of death. But I found myself unprepared for her suffering. Convulsions racked her body; as she became dehydrated, dark hollows deepened around her eyes and cheeks, turning her strong, pretty face into a skeletal mask; her features contorted in an expression of relentless pain. I felt chained to her experience, with no relief, and there were many moments when I truly thought I could no longer bear seeing her in agony. But I was determined to be there for her as she had always been for me.

During Mother's last hours, I laid my head near hers and spoke softly to her. Her breathing became labored as her organs shut down, and panic struck chords in my deepest core. Finally, she inhaled a long breath, and when she did not exhale, I put my arm under her head and pulled her cheek to mine. She died in my arms.

I was asked by my grieving family to write Mother's eulogy but I put it off, just as I was putting off the realization that life must now go on without Mother. I waited until the morning of the funeral to begin. But the words would not come. Still in shock from living through my mother's traumatic dying, I found my thoughts wandering over and over to her final days. I felt some-how I had let her down. She had always "made it better" for me when things went wrong; but I had been helpless in her hour of greatest need.

Slowly, the thought formed that perhaps all I could do now was honor her. But what could I write, short of a novel the size of Texas? I did not want people to hear the banal facts of where she was born, what year she married. I wanted them to see her blue-green eyes, to hear her strong voice, to smell her favorite perfume, to be awed by the knowledge she possessed. The words began to pour out. I sat on the side of my bed, looking out into the woods we had walked so often together, and wrote the entire eulogy without once stopping.

At the funeral, I handed the pages I had written to Brother Headrick and made a quick getaway to the chapel. I needed a few moments alone to collect myself and pray. I knew the minister well. His voice was rich and deep and would do justice to her attributes.

Minutes before the service began the minister appeared to explain that he'd forgotten his glasses. "I can't read a word without them," he said. "I'll need for you to read the eulogy yourself." My mind went blank. I looked at my sister, who was standing beside me, and asked her if she could read it. "Oh, I couldn't," she declined. I turned to my brother, who looked away in tears, shaking his head. Next I asked my cousin, an accomplished speaker. "I'm so sorry, I'd never make it all the way through," he said.

The organ began playing the hymn to start the service. All the terror of my school days flooded back. How could I get up before all these people and speak, especially when I would be sharing my deepest thoughts and my naked pain? But there was no one else to do it. Brother Headrick took my arm, guided me to a chair, and said, "Sit here beside me, and when it's time, I'll give you a nod."

When it was time, I arose and walked to the podium, my shaking hands gripping three handwritten pages. "I cannot in a page or two begin to do justice to the memory of my mother," I read, choking. I looked up from my pages, into the faces of the people who had come to bid my mother farewell. Their faces were filled with sadness. I began to cry, and my voice shook so violently that I was ashamed to speak another word. I squeezed my eyes shut and told myself I had to continue, but as I struggled on, my voice broke like the vibrato of a tragic violin. Once more, from the pages now wet with tears, I glanced up. Tears were streaming down the faces of everyone in the room. They saw the pain I was suffering, and they were suffering with me. Knowing this gave me the strength to keep going.

Days later, my brother told me that my reading of the eulogy was the most courageous thing he had ever witnessed. He is a Vietnam War veteran and has seen much of courage and pain, and I accepted his words like balm on a wound. Perhaps it was courage. It was certainly the hardest thing I have ever done. But I think of it as honor. On that day, remembering all of her I could remember, I would have done anything to honor my mother.

My fear of speaking publicly came to an end that day. There could never be a more difficult moment to speak, never a time I would feel so inadequate and alone. If I could do it then, I could do it anywhere, and I have spoken before audiences many times since then.

Somehow, I know Mother would say, "I knew you could do it!"

Tarzie Hart has won awards for poetry and has been recognized for her short stories. She is a district coordinator for VSA Arts of Missouri, an organization devoted to promoting the creative power of people with disabilities. She is working on her second novel.

> *"Until the day of his death, no man can be sure of his courage."*
> —Jean Anouilh

UPCOMING VOLUMES INCLUDE:

CHARITY: Real Stories of Giving and Receiving
WISDOM: Learning Life's Lessons
HOPE: True Tales of Dreams Fulfilled

If you have an experience that fits one of
these books, you may submit an essay to:

RED ROCK PRESS
Suite 114, 459 Columbus Avenue
New York, New York 10024

Emigrants Crossing the Plains, 1866, by Currier and Ives.

Praise for FORTITUDE: True Stories of True Grit

"These stories will bring you to your feet cheering and to your knees in awe and humility. A compulsively good read."—PAULA M. REEVES, AUTHOR OF *WOMAN'S INTUITION*

"Malinda Teel challenges us to be as courageous and persistent in our struggles as the men and women of today who tell their stories here." —MILLARD FULLER, HABITAT FOR HUMANITY INTERNATIONAL

"These stories, filled with poignancy and uncommon honesty, bring to light what is often hidden: regular people really do commit acts of bravery. A reminder of what greatness actually is."—BEN KAMIN, AUTHOR OF *THE PATH OF THE SOUL*

"These are moving and splendid contemporary models for the old-fashioned virtues of pluck and courage. They provide an inspiration for taking life on full force." —AUGUSTUS Y. NAPIER, COAUTHOR OF *THE FAMILY CRUCIBLE*

Malinda Teel is an Atlanta-based writer and psychotherapist.

$14.95

ISBN 0-9669573-7-7

51495

9 780966 957372

RED ROCK PRESS
New York, New York

www.redrockpress.com